Brando

Brando

A BIOGRAPHY IN PHOTOGRAPHS

by Christopher Nickens

A DOLPHIN BOOK

Doubleday

NEW YORK   1987

Library of Congress Cataloging-in-Publication Data
Nickens, Christopher.
     Brando: a biography in photographs.
     "A Dolphin book."
     1. Brando, Marlon—Portraits.   2. Actors—United
States—Portraits.   I. Title.
PN2287.B683N5   1987   791.43'028'0924   [B]   87-5296
ISBN: 0-385-23308-6

Acknowledgments

For their generous help in the preparation of this book, many thanks to Allison Waldman, Guy Vespoint, Karen Swenson, Vernon Patterson, Morris Everett, Neal Peters, George Zeno, Mary Barton, Ralph Osborn and James Spada.

For sharing their memories of Marlon Brando, I am grateful to Red Buttons, Shirley Jones and Stanley Kramer. Thanks also to the staffs of the libraries of the Academy of Motion Picture Arts and Sciences, the American Film Institute and the University of Southern California.

For their friendship and moral support, affectionate thanks go to Paul O'Driscoll, Jerry Clar, Richard Parker, Paul Rose, Sharon Davis, Lance Benware, Ken de Bie, John Cusimano, Jeff Schaffer, Bruce R. Mandes, Donovan Scott, Karl Nakamura and Gregory Rice. As always, special thanks to Paul Bresnick, Kathy Robbins and Loretta Weingel-Fidel.

Contents

Introduction

When Marlon Brando first captured the public's imagination at the dawn of the 1950s, it was only partly due to his brooding good looks, blatant sex appeal and controversial acting style. In addition to these purely theatrical attributes, Brando was perceived as a symbol of the restlessness and frustration taking hold of America's postwar youth.

Through his roles in such films as *The Men, A Streetcar Named Desire, On the Waterfront* and particularly *The Wild One,* he struck a nerve in millions of young people who were just beginning to question the conformity and restrictive mores of the Eisenhower era. To this ever-growing audience, Brando came to epitomize youthful alienation and rebellion.

In his first few movie roles, he raged against the violence and corruption of the New York dock unions, challenged the hypocrisy of small-town law and order and confronted sexual repression with a dangerous, muscular aggression that had never been seen on film.

Offscreen as well, Brando's irreverent approach to his stardom, his often brutish manners and his refusal to play by time-honored Hollywood rules only contributed to his public image as the quintessential antihero. Never seeking to become the symbol of anything, Marlon suddenly found himself hailed as the mumbling leader of a new breed of iconoclastic artists.

Idolatry was something Brando never encouraged and he was puzzled by the public's reaction to him and the lofty status granted to actors in general. Over the years he has consistently pooh-poohed his talent and the regard in which he is held by fellow performers. "There are no artists," he once declared. "We are businessmen. We're merchants. There is no art."

Marlon also realized that there was danger in being singled out as the vanguard of a particular movement or generation. There is always the very real possibility that as an era passes, so too might the appeal of those artists chosen to symbolize it. To some degree, this did indeed happen to Brando in the midsixties. A spate of poor films rendered him slightly passé and the public regarded him, perhaps unfairly, as just another overpaid movie star: the rebel had gone Establishment.

Ironically, this professional slump was concurrent with Brando's controversial, highly visible stand on such then-unpopular—even radical—issues as civil rights for blacks and American Indians. In his personal life, at least, he had never been more of a rebel.

By 1970 Brando's career was in such peril that critics and fans alike despaired of his future in films. He was spending more and more time away from the camera, living in seclusion on his private South Pacific island: there seemed to be few acting challenges left.

Just two years later, however, he startled the doomsayers with his now-mythic performance as the title character in *The Godfather*. The film was a massive critical and financial hit and Brando followed it with equally brilliant work in the controversial *Last Tango in Paris*. Via this one-two punch, he reestablished his prominence within an industry that had all but written him off. It was a classic, irresistible Hollywood comeback.

Subsequent career choices—some made strictly for money—have again proven disappointing, but this is nothing new in Brando's career. To be sure, for whatever motivation, Marlon has appeared in his share of inferior productions, often testing the loyalty of even his most ardent admirers. Like all enduring stars, he has balanced hits with misses. But his truly magnificent performances—and there are more than a few—make up the foundation of his revered position as one of the most influential acting talents of all time.

For Barbra Streisand, who found inspiration in Marlon Brando's talents and who, in turn, has inspired others.

He loves the light! See how the light shines through him? . . . I shouldn't be partial, but he is my favorite one.

Tennessee Williams,
The Glass Menagerie

I

Beginnings

1924–1949

At fifteen, Marlon Brando, Jr., boasted to his classmates at Township High School in Libertyville, Illinois, "I'll be famous someday. I'll come back to Libertyville and the mayor will greet me at the station. There'll be a big parade. Flags will be flying, the band will be playing and everybody will be shouting, 'Welcome home, Brando!'" A typical adolescent declaration—except that in Marlon's case everyone apparently agreed with him.

"That boy had something different from the rest of us," recalled one high school sweetheart. "When you talked with him, you just knew he was going places. The odd thing was that he knew it too." Shortly after Brando won his first Oscar in 1955, his sister Frances told reporters, "Yes, he's still the same . . . the only difference is that he's famous now. But that's no surprise. We sort of expected it."

The personal charisma and complex mix of personality traits that combined to make Marlon Brando an artist of rare quality as well as a provocative public figure were in evidence even in his earliest years. It wasn't that his acting talent was recognized while he was a child—although he did entertain the neighborhood with imitations of radio newscasters—but simply that there was something special about Marlon that set him apart. He was born on April 3, 1924, in Omaha, Nebraska, to Dorothy Pennebaker Brando and Marlon Sr. He was their third child—their only son—and was nicknamed Bud. Marlon's parents were usually poles apart on any given subject, but they were particularly at odds regarding their son's upbringing.

Marlon Sr. was the archetypal post-Victorian father figure: taciturn, conservative and difficult—sometimes impossible—to please. Characterized as "relentlessly masculine," he was determined that his son grow up in his image. He encouraged Bud to hunt, box, fish and try out for school athletics. With his sturdy build and natural grace, the boy excelled in most of these endeavors, though he seldom heard a word of praise from his demanding father. "Nothing I ever did interested or satisfied him," Brando once admitted with bitterness.

In contrast, Dorothy Brando was open-minded and progressive in her approach to motherhood. She instilled in her children a love of art, literature and especially drama. She had, in fact, enjoyed an intermittent career as an amateur actress, performing in local productions of *Liliom, Pygmalion* and *Anna Christie.* Dorothy's children adored her and learned to accept her inability to stand up to her domineering husband—and later her alcoholism. The distinct, disparate personalities of his parents naturally influenced young Marlon, but he seems to have started developing a multifaceted persona all his own at a very young age. Some armchair analysts have suggested that the celebrated Brando

concern for human rights might have begun as early as his ninth year when he brought home (on more than one occasion) out-of-work transients for a bowl of his mother's soup.

But the wicked—sometimes nasty—sense of humor that has either delighted or outraged Marlon's associates over the years also began in childhood. Wally Cox, a boyhood pal who would remain close to Brando until his death, recalls a game of cowboys and Indians in which Marlon tied Cox to a tree and left him there overnight. This interesting combination of thoughtful sensitivity and almost mean-spirited prankishness (mixed with good looks and a flair for the dramatic) set Marlon apart from the other kids, who felt—as Marlon did—that he was marked for future greatness.

ABOVE: The Brando siblings. Three-year-old Marlon is held in place by Jocelyn, age six, while Frances, five, poses on the right.

3

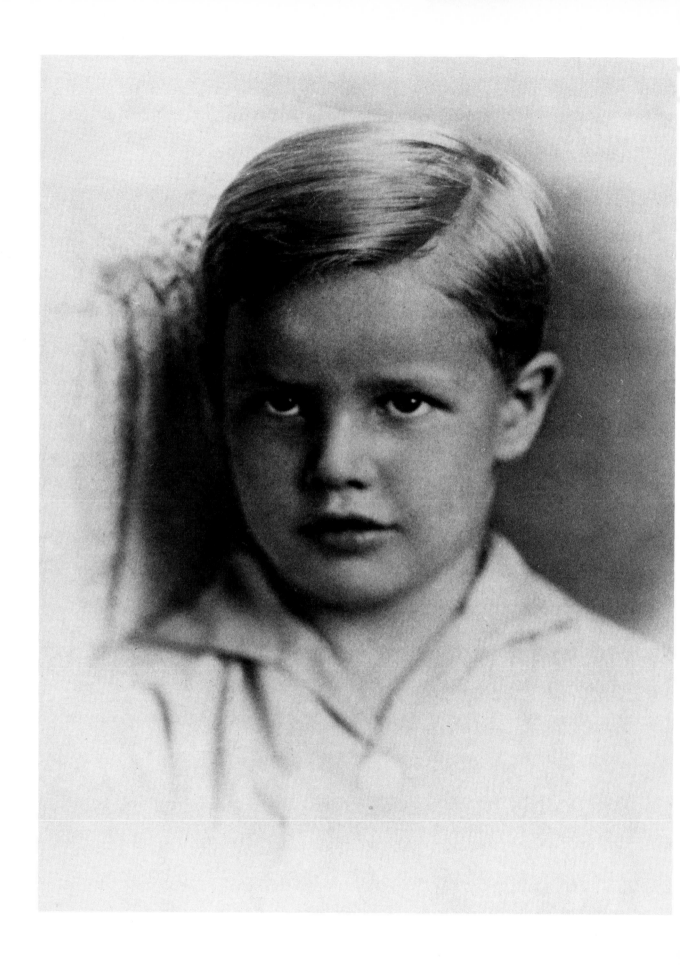

OPPOSITE: Marlon at five. The angelic face belied a pugnacious nature the boy developed as a defense against neighborhood bullies who taunted him about his fancy-sounding name. "Brando" had been derived from the French "Brandeau" and, combined with Marlon, it would prove to be wonderful for a future show business career, but it was a shade too exotic for Marlon's playmates in 1930 Omaha.

ABOVE: Marlon is in the front row, extreme right, in this class photo taken in Evanston, Illinois, where the Brandos had moved following Marlon's sixth birthday. Marlon Sr.'s sales career forced the family to relocate several times during this period. From Evanston they moved to Santa Ana, California, for two years, then on to Minnesota for a brief stay. Finally they returned to Illinois, settling in Libertyville.

No matter what the locale, attending school did little to alter Marlon's independent, moody behavior. He was extremely bright, but lazy, and had to be coaxed to apply himself to his studies. Bored with most subjects, he was often caught daydreaming in class. He did like music, however, taking up the drums in homage to his idol, swing drummer Gene Krupa. Marlon's defiant streak became more pronounced as he reached adolescence. Once, peeved with a particular teacher, he handed in a homework assignment written entirely on toilet paper.

mencement play was canceled when Marlon was expelled; he was to have starred in the production and a suitable replacement could not be found.

Marlon's expulsion from Shattuck had nothing to do with the cherry bomb incident. He was dismissed when he left campus to visit Faribault during an important government inspection.

OPPOSITE: The baby face had matured into striking handsomeness by the time this portrait was taken shortly before Marlon set off for New York and a career in the theater.

Unlike most of his peers, Marlon was not forced to fight in World War II. Ironically, it was his stint at Shattuck that kept Brando out of the service. During a football game at the school, he suffered a knee injury that resulted in his being classified 4-F.

After leaving Shattuck, Brando returned to Libertyville with no definite plans for the future. He declined his father's offer to join the family insecticide business and after a short career as a ditchdigger Marlon chose to join his sisters in Manhattan. (Jocelyn had enrolled in the American Academy of Dramatic Arts, while Frances was studying at the Art Students League.) Marlon Sr. agreed grudgingly to finance his son's acting aspirations, but only for six months. If Marlon hadn't established at least the beginnings of a career at the end of that time, he was to return home and join his father's business.

ABOVE: In the fall of 1941, Marlon enrolled in the Shattuck School, a military academy located outside Faribault, Minnesota. His father, an alumnus, hoped that the Shattuck regimen would build a sense of personal discipline in his unruly son.

Marlon was, predictably, hardly a model student during his year and a half at Shattuck, but neither was he the hell-raiser the Brando myth would have him be. For years tales of his outrageous exploits have been repeated as gospel: chamber pots tossed out windows at cadets, ropes cut so that tower bells plunged through classroom roofs and cherry bombs set off at an instructor's door, resulting in his expulsion.

In reality, Brando's worst infringements seem to have been smoking, chronic lateness and feigned illness. The closest he came to outrageousness was bleaching his hair white-blond for the amusement of his classmates. "Brando was likable, he was a good boy and there was not a bit of the malicious in him," recalled his history teacher in 1956. "But Brando and Shattuck *were* incompatible," he added.

Another myth is that he showed no interest in acting at the school. "He was without question the finest drama student I have ever known," said the head of the English department. In fact, the com-

ABOVE: An unusual study of Brando taken at the start of his career. Soon after he arrived in New York in the summer of 1943, Marlon took Jocelyn's advice and enrolled in the Dramatic Workshop of the New School for Social Research. Under the tutelage of Stella Adler—and later Lee Strasberg—he found himself in the home of a controversial acting ideology derived from the teachings of the Russian theater innovator Konstantin Stanislavsky. Strasberg later founded The Actors Studio, a workshop for professionals, which followed the same formula.

Known simplistically as "the Method," this technique called for the actor to (among other things) reach deep within his own experience, often calling on personal memories both painful and joyous, to better understand and convey the motivations of a particular character. Brando took easily to the tenets of this performance concept, but he never would have imagined during his first months at the New School that within a few short years he would become the Method's most conspicuous proponent. Stella Adler was immediately impressed with Brando and told her associates, including Strasberg, "This puppy thing [Brando] will be the best young actor on the American stage."

OPPOSITE: A coy portrait taken by Cecil Beaton. During his first year in Manhattan, Marlon moved constantly from one small apartment to another, rooming for a while with his boyhood friend Wally Cox. Cox worked as a silversmith at the time, but later turned to performing—at Brando's urging—and went on to fame as television's "Mr. Peepers." Cox said of Brando in 1944, "Marlon is a creative philosopher, a very deep thinker. He's a liberating source for his friends."

Indeed, Brando was not above liberating rent money from his friends in a pinch and he also panhandled occasionally. He viewed talking strangers out of their pocket money as a challenge, an acting exercise. Marlon first appeared on the New York stage in several productions (including *Twelfth Night* and two Molière plays) for the New School at the Adelphia Theater. Following a summer of similar acting assignments in Sayville, New York, he was cast in his first Broadway show, John Van Druten's *I Remember Mama*.

LEFT: *I Remember Mama* is a homey comedy-drama about a family of Norwegian immigrants in 1910 San Francisco. Marlon—here with cast members including Mady Christians (top left) and Frances Heflin (bottom left)—was paid $75 a week for his performance as Nels. The part was not showy and little attention was paid Brando by critics following the play's opening at the Music Box Theater in October 1944. Audiences, however, responded to Marlon's charismatic stage presence and noisily flipped through their programs to learn his identity the minute he made his first entrance.

Except for his name, though, Brando's short bio in *Playbill* was useless to curious theatergoers. "Born in Calcutta, India," it stated, "where his father was engaged in geological research, he came to this country when he was six months old." With this playful piece of fiction, Marlon began a lifelong stance of defiance regarding personal publicity. He didn't believe in it as a means to further his career. "The only thing an actor owes the public," he once declared, "is not to bore them." Marlon's fanciful biography varied only slightly for most of his stage appearances. For a spring 1946 production of *Candida* with Katharine Cornell, Marlon claimed he "was born in Bangkok while his father was engaged in zoological research."

ABOVE: Marlon stayed with *I Remember Mama* for a year, surviving several cast changes. He acquired his first agent during the run of the play, but was unsuccessful in an attempt to impress New York representatives of the movie industry. "You wouldn't photograph well," one studio scout told him. "Your nose dribbles down your face like ice cream." Brando was philosophical about such rejection. He said around this time, "I'd like to be in a good picture sometime, but I'm never going to be a movie star in the strict sense of the word. I don't want to be an Alan Ladd and have that bobby sox crowd around me. I'd rather shoot myself."

ABOVE: Ann Shepherd and Marlon enjoy a rare light moment from *Truckline Cafe,* Brando's second Broadway production, which opened in February 1946 at the Belasco Theater. This Maxwell Anderson creation about a group of unsavory characters in a California diner struggling through postwar neuroses received scathing reviews and closed after thirteen performances. Marlon was cast as a homecoming veteran who kills his wife (Shepherd) after learning of her infidelities. His performance brought him his first good notices. "It was Marlon Brando who walked away with the show," wrote George Freedley in the *Morning Telegraph,* "with his brilliant portrayal of the deceived husband. His scene of anguish after killing his wife was really terrific and he deserved every round of applause his exit earned."

Hollywood began showing interest in Brando as a result of his work in *Truckline Cafe.* The first screenplay of *Rebel Without a Cause* was floating around New York at the time and Marlon was approached by Warner Brothers about starring in it. The project fell through and when *Rebel* emerged with James Dean in the lead a decade later, it bore little resemblance to the story Brando had been considered for. Legend states that Marlon actually made a screen test at this time, but it has never been tracked down and Brando has remained mute on the subject.

RIGHT: A moment from *Truckline Cafe.* New York critics and certain Hollywood scouts may have taken notice of Brando, but he was still, after three years, just another struggling young actor. Surely one reason he didn't work more was the unorthodox approach he took with interviews and auditions —which he felt, for the most part, were beneath him. His condescending attitude, his fondness for wearing nothing but Levi's and undershirts and his unwillingness to read a script "cold" did nothing to endear him to prospective employers.

He once astonished Alfred Lunt and Lynne Fontanne during an audition for their production of *O Mistress Mine* when he walked onstage, absently held the script, stared into space and said nothing for several long moments, then left. In response to the script for Noel Coward's drawing room comedy *Present Laughter,* he returned a note to the author that said: "Don't you know there are people in the world starving?"

Fortunately for Marlon, he met several important talents during this period, such as Elia Kazan and Stanley Kramer, who would remember him for future projects.

OPPOSITE: A portrait from Marlon's next stage appearance in *A Flag Is Born*, which opened at the Alvin Theater in September 1946. Brando costarred with one of his acting heroes, Paul Muni, in this propagandistic Ben Hecht play about Britain's postwar involvement in the Holy Land. Marlon played an outspoken, cynical Jewish soldier who encounters two fervent Zionists (Muni and Celia Adler) in a graveyard outside Palestine. *A Flag Is Born* was criticized for its political naïveté and Muni was called "hammy," but Marlon was singled out for his "commanding presence." During the run of this little-seen play, Brando turned down an offer from Elia Kazan to star in the 20th Century-Fox production of *Gentleman's Agreement*.

In December 1946 Marlon signed to star opposite Tallulah Bankhead in Jean Cocteau's *The Eagle Has Two Heads*. Although the play was not well-suited to Brando's talents—it is a talky fantasy involving an Austrian Queen's paranoia about her possible assassination—he realized that costarring with the redoubtable Bankhead would bring him his greatest public exposure to date.

The Eagle Has Two Heads was a fiasco from the outset. Brando mumbled his way through rehearsals, planning to save himself for performances. Bankhead made no secret of her contempt for Method actors and complained loudly about Marlon's "boorishness." Brando refused to bow and scrape to Tallulah, whom he considered a personality rather than a serious actress. After Marlon upstaged Bankhead during the play's first performance, he was fired. It was announced that Brando, at twenty-two, was not believable as a lover to Bankhead, then forty-four. Within weeks of his dismissal, Marlon was sent a script by Elia Kazan for a new drama by Tennessee Williams: *A Streetcar Named Desire*.

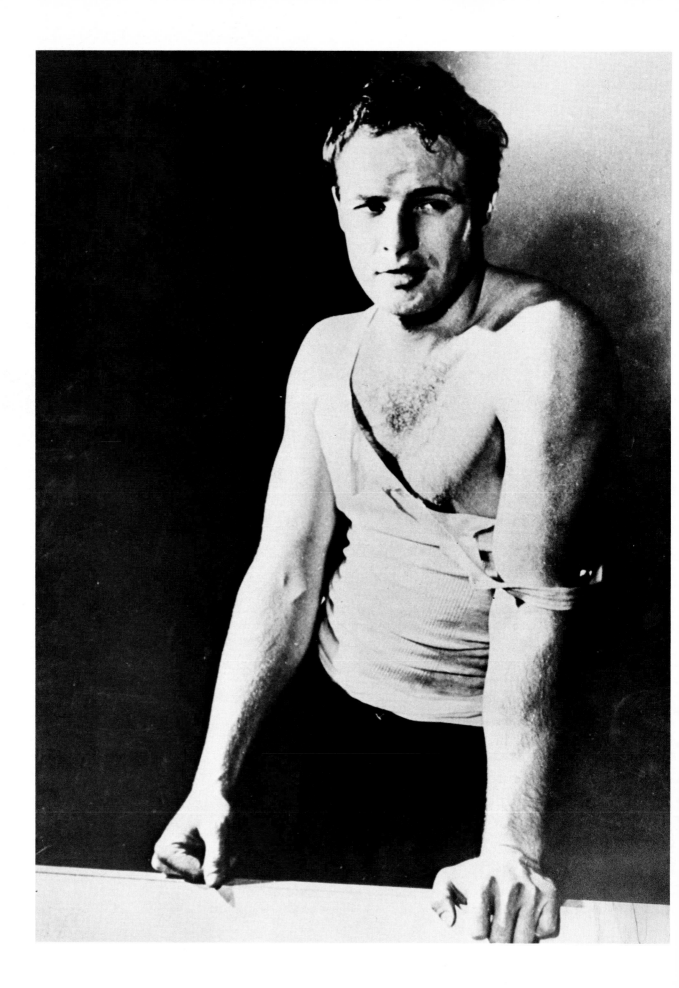

OPPOSITE: Complete with torn T-shirt, Marlon portrays Stanley Kowalski, the role that brought him Broadway fame and screen immortality in *A Streetcar Named Desire*. Typical of so many "big break" tales, Brando was not the first or even the second actor wanted for this watershed part. Elia Kazan had signed John Garfield, but the actor left the production after Tennessee Williams refused to enlarge the Kowalski role. Only after prior commitments kept Burt Lancaster from taking on Stanley did Kazan send the script to Brando's agent. In contrast to Garfield's feelings, Brando initially considered the role "a size too large for me." After he thought it over, however, Marlon agreed to play Kowalski—primarily because he trusted Kazan.

Brando's casting had to be approved by Tennessee Williams. To save time, Marlon was sent by bus to the playwright's Cape Cod bungalow. He immediately endeared himself to Williams by unclogging a stubborn sink drain and replacing a fuse—tasks Williams found impossible. Marlon then proceeded to read *Streetcar* aloud for Williams and his guests. As if onstage, Brando brought Kowalski thrillingly to life. He was by turns crudely sexual and arrogant, insensitive and demanding and finally childlike in his bellowing for his wife Stella's attention. He was immediately cast in the play.

On *Streetcar*'s opening night—December 3, 1947 —Marlon received a now-famous wire from Tennessee Williams: RIDE OUT BOY AND SEND IT BACK SOLID. FROM THE GREASY POLACK YOU WILL SOMEDAY ARRIVE AT THE GLOOMY DANE. FOR YOU HAVE SOMETHING THAT MAKES THE THEATER A WORLD OF GREAT POSSIBILITIES.

ABOVE: Brando as Stanley, Kim Hunter as Stella Kowalski and Jessica Tandy as Blanche du Bois in *A Streetcar Named Desire*. Set in the slums of New Orleans, *Streetcar* is an achingly true portrait of a faded Southern belle (du Bois) and her gradual descent into madness, exacerbated by a rape at the hands of her loutish brother-in-law, Stanley. Arguably Tennessee Williams's finest work, *Streetcar* is an acting tour de force. On paper, it is the wistful, pathetic and ultimately tragic Blanche that offers the greatest acting challenge, but Stanley also requires a performer of immense skill. Further, the Kowalski role calls for a powerful stage presence and sexual magnetism.

Brando was inspired casting for the play and he earned wonderful reviews. The *Journal-American* raved, "Brando is our theater's most memorable actor at his most memorable." Adjectives such as "magnificent," "powerful," "courageous" and "astonishing" were hurled Marlon's way in the press and Jessica Tandy's notices were even better. *Streetcar* won every possible award as the play of the year and reaffirmed Tennessee Williams's position as the country's most important new playwright. It also changed Marlon Brando's life.

ABOVE: *A Streetcar Named Desire* ran for eighteen months to packed houses. To break the monotony, Marlon would vary his performance from night to night and sometimes from scene to scene. Kim Hunter recalled in a 1962 interview, "It is a tremendous experience to play in relationship to Brando; he yanks you into his own sense of reality. For example . . . the way Marlon played the scene where Stanley goes through Blanche's trunk. Stanley has found out a little bit about her at that point in the play and is starting to question her. He begins to go through the things in her trunk while Stella tries to protect her sister's belongings.

"Marlon never, never did that scene the same way twice during the entire run. He had a different sort of attitude toward each of the belongings every night; sometimes it would lead me into getting into quite a fight with him and other times I'd be seeing him as a silly little boy. I got worn-out after many months in the play, but I never got bored."

Marlon got bored, and like a "silly little boy" he played pranks on his coworkers. With his back to the audience, he would make faces and stick his tongue out at Jessica Tandy during her most difficult scenes. By the end of the run, she refused to even speak to him.

Just before curtain one night, Marlon broke his nose during backstage horseplay with his under-study Jack Palance. He went on in great pain, but never bothered to have the break set properly. His new profile was less beautiful, but more interesting —and, in his eyes, more manly.

OPPOSITE: A dramatic study of Marlon Brando, Broadway star. With his success in *Streetcar*, Marlon found that his personal and professional life had become fodder for the gossip columns. He was flattered when paid a compliment about a performance, but he couldn't fathom the crowds of young women clustered around his stage door every evening. Worst of all, the enthusiastic attention paid to Brando at every turn helped put an end to his first serious New York romance (to Puerto Rican fashion plate Cecilia D'Artuniaga) and forced him to move out of his small West Side apartment when the address became common knowledge.

On the plus side, Marlon was earning $500 a week—sending $400 home to his father to invest— and receiving tantalizing offers from Hollywood. After *A Streetcar Named Desire* closed, Brando journeyed to Paris for an extended rest. On the verge of making his first film, he reflected upon the strangeness of stardom, his ambivalent emotions about it and how it might affect his future as an actor and as a person.

II

Rebel Superstar
1950–1953

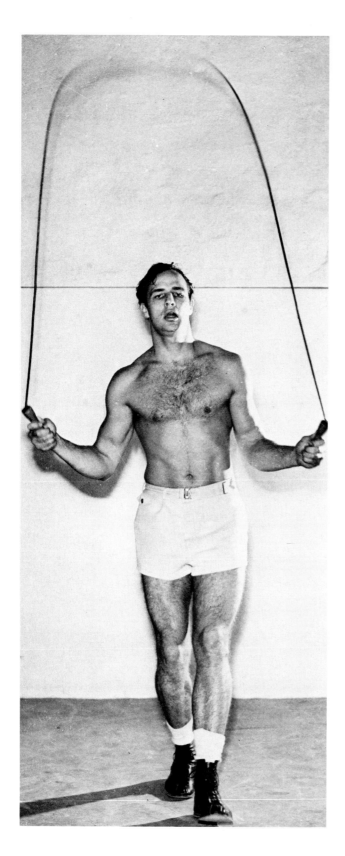

LEFT: In one of his first Hollywood publicity photos, Marlon gets into shape for his film debut in *The Men.* Producer Stanley Kramer, known for his socially relevant dramas *Champion* and *Home of the Brave,* had seen Brando play the anguished veteran in *Truckline Cafe* and felt he would be ideal as the embittered paraplegic vet in *The Men.* Typically, Brando agreed to the project as much for what it had to say about the plight of physically and emotionally injured soldiers returning to a sometimes indifferent society as for the dramatic possibilities of an unusual role.

In preparation to play a man who is wheelchairbound for most of the film, Marlon moved into a Southern California veteran's hospital for over a month to better understand his character's condition. Such dedication was rare in Hollywood and it was immediately labeled the Method approach at its most extreme.

In a further move against Tinseltown tradition, Brando refused glamorous bachelor digs at the Beverly Hills Hotel in favor of his Aunt Betty's small home in the blue-collar Los Angeles suburb of Eagle Rock. When word got out that this handsome, acclaimed, about-to-be star slept on his aunt's sofa for the duration of *The Men* production (with a pet raccoon named Russell at his side), it was agreed that in a town loaded with eccentrics Marlon Brando would be worth watching.

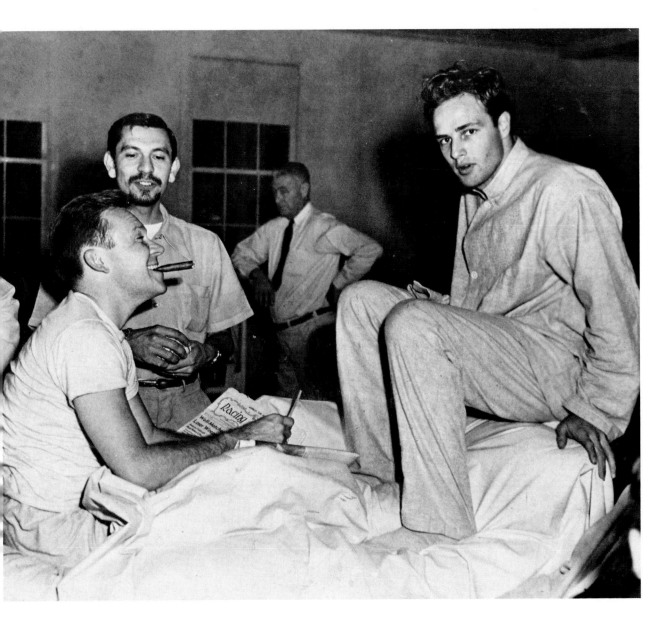

ABOVE: A candid conversation between costars Jack Webb (standing), Marlon and Richard Erdman on the hospital set of *The Men.* With his reputation as a highly charged emotional actor preceding him, Brando baffled his coworkers when he stuck to his stage tradition and walked through rehearsals. But the moment the cameras rolled, he delivered solidly. There was little of the awkwardness seen so often in stage-trained screen newcomers.

Stanley Kramer explains. "He was very comfortable right away. He was so bathed in preoccupation with the fact that he'd been living at the hospital for so long and became so well-versed with the paraplegia and the wheelchair that he was oblivious to the camera."

It may have looked that way, but Brando admitted that he found the experience of film acting difficult. "It is the toughest form of acting," he said in 1952. "And anyone who can come through it successfully can call himself an actor for the first time. When you have to portray a shattering emotion while realizing at the back of your mind that if you move your head an inch too much, you'll be out of focus and out of frame . . . that's acting."

ABOVE: In *The Men*, Marlon's character Ken overcomes his bitter self-pity with the help of his doting fiancée, played by Teresa Wright, seen with him here. In his first screen romance, Brando was allowed to show a vulnerable, sensitive quality that would be rare in his first films as a major star. A veteran of ten years in the movies, Wright told a visitor to the set that Marlon had reduced her to unplanned tears during his reading of several speeches and that he "is probably the most exciting young actor to appear in pictures in ages. He will have a wonderful career."

OPPOSITE: An unusual portrait taken to publicize *The Men.* When it opened in July 1950, the film was praised for its sincere intentions, but it was not a success. Stanley Kramer believes that the outbreak of the Korean War, just as the picture went into wide release, ruined its box office potential. A public being called to arms wasn't interested in a story that was essentially antiwar.

Nor did *The Men* make an overnight star of Marlon Brando. In spite of some excellent, insightful reviews (one British critic labeled Marlon's appeal "radical masculinity"), Brando was primarily greeted as an interesting new face with potential for full-fledged stardom.

As he did following every film for the next decade, Marlon returned to New York after completing *The Men.* When United Artists approached him later to publicize the picture, they often got more than they bargained for. He grunted through an interview with Hedda Hopper and refused to even see Louella Parsons, whom he dubbed "the fat one." When another reporter began an interview by declaring that she didn't find his looks "so hot," he clammed up, walked to a nearby corner and stood on his head until the woman left the room. When asked by a studio publicist if there was anything he could do for Marlon during a brief visit to Chicago, Brando replied, "Yeah. Can you tell me where I can get my raccoon fucked?"

OPPOSITE: In the summer of 1950, Marlon began filming *A Streetcar Named Desire* for Warner Brothers under the guidance of Elia Kazan. Although *The Men* had failed to set any box office records, it proved conclusively that Brando was as magnetic on-screen as he had been onstage, so there was no opposition when Kazan insisted that Brando re-create his Stanley Kowalski in the movie version of *Streetcar*.

ABOVE: Vivien Leigh, Marlon and Kim Hunter pause for lunch on the *Streetcar* set. With all of the principal roles cast from stage productions (Leigh had starred for eight months as Blanche du Bois in the London company), Kazan had a relatively easy task directing actors who were extremely familiar with the demands of their characters.

With Brando already labeled "Hollywood's New Bad Boy" and Vivien Leigh noted for her erratic mental stability, a flare-up between the two stars seemed inevitable. But setside gossips were disappointed when, after an initial period of awkwardness, Leigh and Brando became fast friends. Vivien recognized genius when she saw it and she confided to Kazan that working opposite Marlon brought out facets of her du Bois characterization she hadn't touched on before. Likewise, Brando admitted to having been always "terrifically impressed" with Leigh's talent and he was pleased to find her ladylike but not stuffy. He was also surprised and delighted by Vivien's unexpected off-color vocabulary.

27

ABOVE: What would cocky Stanley Kowalski think of Marlon's intense interest in Kim Hunter's knitting? For all of the seriousness of the screenplay he was filming, Brando couldn't resist indulging in adolescent stunts occasionally. One time after Hunter retired to her dressing room for a nap, Marlon waited for her to fall asleep, then shook her trailer violently and shouted, "Earthquake!" He was also fond of terrorizing the *Streetcar* company with a huge fake black spider he had acquired during a weekend trip to Tijuana.

OPPOSITE: Tennessee Williams's classic adversaries Blanche du Bois and Stanley Kowalski in *A Streetcar Named Desire*, which opened to tremendous critical acclaim in the fall of 1951. In spite of a few script changes to please the still-powerful censors (the young man Blanche loved in her youth, for example, could not be identified as a homosexual), the film was credited with almost single-handedly ushering in a new era of frankness in American films.

Shortly after the premiere, Kazan, with no trace of false modesty, said, "It is a landmark. Its issues are not oversimplified and you're not in there 'rooting for somebody'—all that old shit the motion picture industry is built upon. There is no hero or heroine; the people are people—some dross, some gold, with faults and virtues . . . and for a while you are muddled about them, the way you would be in life."

Although considered controversial by some, *Streetcar* found enough favor with the Hollywood Establishment to win a slew of Oscar nominations. It lost "Best Picture" to *An American in Paris* and while Leigh, Hunter and Karl Malden—as Blanche's suitor—all won Academy Awards, Brando was passed over in favor of Humphrey Bogart, a sentimental and deserving choice for his work in *The African Queen*. For years after its debut, *A Streetcar Named Desire* wielded a strong influence over the filmmaking community; everything about it was emulated for years with varying success. Alex North's bluesy, evocative score, for example, was copied in dozens of sexy fifties potboilers.

OPPOSITE: Losing the Oscar hardly mattered to Brando's career. His riveting, completely original performance in *Streetcar* thrust him into immediate superstardom. Within weeks of the picture's release, everyone from school kids to nightclub comics was paying tribute to Stanley Kowalski, screwing up their faces, tearing at imaginary T-shirts and screaming, "Stella! . . . Stella!"

In a more serious vein, Marlon became the most analyzed actor in Hollywood history. The East Coast intelligentsia pondered his Method, his impact on the future of screen acting and on society as a whole. Popular magazines concentrated on his sexual allure.

Brando was recognized as the most exciting male sex symbol in years. In the tradition of Valentino and Gable, Marlon—in the guise of Kowalski—brought a blunt, horny, dangerous quality to his onscreen lovemaking. Some sociologists were alarmed at the response he generated in women, while others welcomed his honesty.

Marlon was annoyed by the public's perception of him as a hunk, especially since the image was derived from Kowalski, who was, after all, a rapist. In fact, Brando found little to like in the "greasy Polack" who brought him such fame. "Kowalski was always right, never afraid," he said. "He never wondered, never doubted himself. His ego was very secure. And he had the kind of brutal aggressiveness I hate. I detest the character."

ABOVE: During a brief stay in Manhattan early in 1952, Marlon is the center of attention as he leaves a Broadway theater. As the screen's newest, most reluctant heartthrob, Brando found he was an idol to the "bobby sox crowd" he had joked about just a few years earlier as an unknown actor.

ABOVE: Soon Marlon was back in Hollywood to work again with Elia Kazan on *Viva Zapata!* for 20th Century-Fox. From a screenplay by John Steinbeck, the film traces the rise and fall of Emiliano Zapata, an outlaw-hero who led a small band of men in an uprising against corrupt land barons in 1910 Mexico.

To suggest Zapata's Indian ancestry, Brando had his nose thickened, eyelids slightly slanted and hair and eyebrows darkened. He also donned a fake mustache. He refused, however, to wear a $500 pair of uncomfortable contact lenses when he saw that his gray-blue eyes would pass for brown in the black-and-white film. Marlon's *Zapata* makeup, the first of several elaborate guises he would adopt during his career, is more obvious in still photographs than it is on film.

BELOW: Jean Peters played Josefa, Zapata's ambitious wife, who urges her husband to take his revolution farther than he had ever dreamed. He eventually assumes the presidency, but is assassinated by long-standing enemies of his cause.

In a departure from the lovemaking techniques of Stanley Kowalski, Brando's Zapata tempers his sexual demands with tenderness—and even a touch of the poetic. "I believe a man is fire and a woman is fuel," he declares to Josefa as he gently strokes her forearm and caresses her fingers in a subtle yet erotic moment. Director Kazan stated that such nonscripted bits of business were almost entirely Brando's idea. "He had an unerring sense of what would be truthful in physical terms," said Kazan. "Sometimes even the smallest gesture became compelling."

ABOVE: Brando's physique was shown to good advantage—though never exploitatively—in *Viva Zapata!*, furthering his status as a sex symbol whether he liked it or not.

As usual, during the making of *Zapata*, Marlon couldn't help but get into mischief. On location in Texas, he shot off a string of firecrackers in a hotel lobby, serenaded Jean Peters from a treetop at three in the morning, horrified cast and crew by playing dead for several minutes following the hail of gunfire that ends Zapata's life and gleefully told visiting reporters that he once ate grasshoppers and gazelle eyes.

It was also while on the Texas location that Marlon first met his future wife Movita Castenada, who had a bit part in the picture. She was only one of several Mexican girls Brando dated during this time, but when she chose to follow Marlon back to Hollywood their romance heated up. Movita had achieved some fame in Mexico as a cabaret performer, but she was known, if at all, to American film audiences as Clark Gable's native-girl love interest in *Mutiny on the Bounty*. She had been seventeen when cast in the 1935 production.

BELOW: An almost comical study of Marlon as Emiliano Zapata. There was nothing funny, however, about the critical and public response to Brando's third film. It was a financial hit and garnered excellent reviews. The London *Times* said, "Brando gives a performance of compelling power which confirms the impression he gave in *Streetcar* of being one of the very few real screen personalities to emerge from America since the war." Marlon was again nominated for an Academy Award, but lost to Gary Cooper for *High Noon*.

Following *Zapata*, Brando decided to accept an MGM offer to play Mark Antony in a John Houseman production of *Julius Caesar*. It was a surprising decision, since Marlon had once stated to Lee Strasberg that he wasn't interested in attempting the classical roles, and he knew he would be at risk of becoming a conspicuous Hollywood laughingstock.

Despite the Oscar nominations and reams of press clippings that hailed Marlon as the greatest new film actor, he had loud detractors as well. Some highly regarded critics were immune to the Brando magic; they saw him only as a brooding, mumbling slob and predicted that his nasal delivery would desecrate Shakespeare's prose.

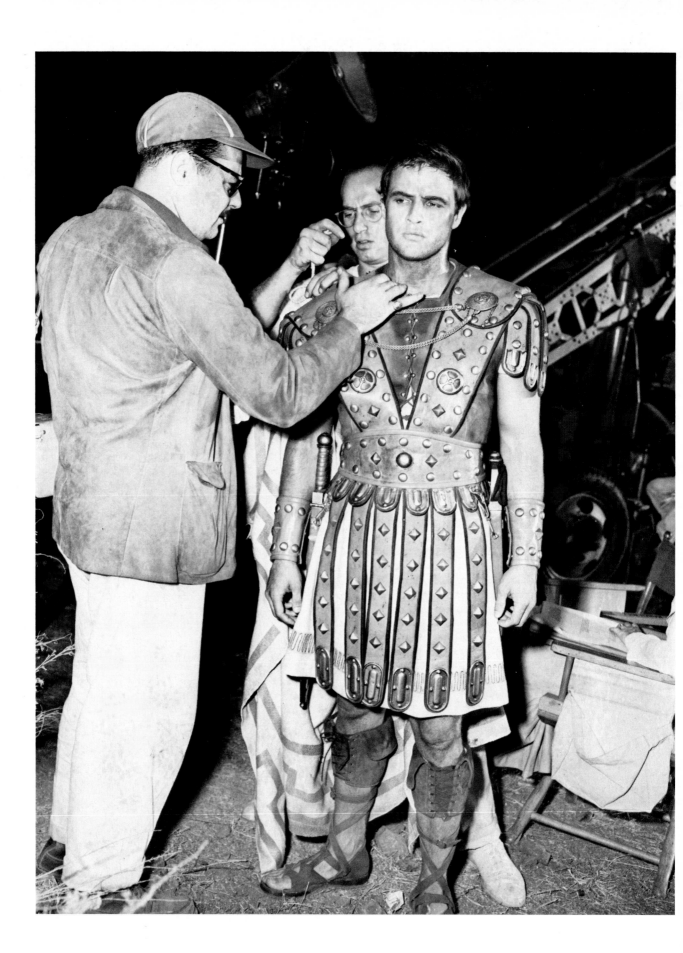

OPPOSITE: Marlon submits to a last-minute costume check before stepping in front of the camera on the *Julius Caesar* set. As it turned out, even MGM chief Dore Schary was skeptical about Brando doing Shakespeare. Director Joseph Mankiewicz was forced to record Marlon delivering two of Mark Antony's speeches as a sort of unofficial audition. Schary was impressed with the audio tapes and Brando was signed for the picture.

ABOVE RIGHT: Out of costume, Marlon is photographed on location for one of *Julius Caesar*'s battle scenes. Candids such as this were often used in fan magazines to stress Brando's sex appeal. The accompanying article might feature a headline such as BRAINY, BRAWNY, BRANDO!

BELOW RIGHT: Brando and Mankiewicz block out the staging for Mark Antony's most famous impassioned oration ("Friends, Romans, countrymen, lend me your ears . . ."), which is delivered to the Roman throngs following Caesar's assassination. At the conclusion of this speech—following eight takes—Marlon received a rousing ovation from fellow cast members John Gielgud, James Mason, Deborah Kerr and Greer Garson. Indeed, Brando was held in high esteem by his traditionally trained coworkers; Gielgud went so far as to offer him a position in repertory at Hammersmith, the prestigious British academy Gielgud headed at the time.

OPPOSITE: *Julius Caesar* was released in the late summer of 1953 to surprisingly good box office and fine reviews. *Variety* declared, "Any fears about Brando appearing in Shakespeare are dispelled by his compelling portrayal as the revengeful Mark Antony . . . he turns in the performance of his career." Marlon was pleased by his good notices for *Julius Caesar* and the Oscar nomination his work earned, but he never attempted another classical role.

His success with Shakespeare did little to alter Brando's eccentric public image. He was now seen more often in sports jackets than jeans and a T-shirt, but was still considered the leading nonconformist of his profession. It was an image he felt was highly exaggerated. "I don't know what people expect when they meet me," he complained at the time. "They seem to be afraid that I'm going to piss in the potted palm and slap them on the ass. Can't they get used to the fact that I'm a human being?"

Marlon's next film only expanded on his image as a rebel, but it would also prove to be one of his most indelible screen appearances.

ABOVE RIGHT: Brando in his quintessential anti-Establishment role as Johnny, leader of the Black Rebels motorcycle gang in *The Wild One*. Based on an explosive true story originally published in *Harper's*, *The Wild One* tells the unsettling tale of two rival gangs whose terrifying invasion of a typical small town results in chaos and, eventually, a man's death. The film reunited Brando with producer Stanley Kramer and was shot in just twenty-four days at Columbia Pictures' San Fernando Valley Ranch.

BELOW RIGHT: Marlon entertains his sister Jocelyn during her visit to the set of *The Wild One*. While her brother's career had skyrocketed, Jocelyn had been working consistently in the New York theater and early East Coast television productions, but with less than spectacular results. She would later appear in roles of varying size in the Brando vehicles *The Ugly American* and *The Chase*.

ABOVE LEFT: Fifteen years before anyone dreamed of *Easy Rider*, Brando, Stanley Kramer and director Laslo Benedek turned out the first "biker flick." It was not something anyone involved in the film originally intended to do. Kramer recalls, "The ironic point of the film was that this town, which had been ravaged by the motorcyclists, never preferred charges because they wanted them back, they brought so much business to the town. Now, that was the irony of the situation, which we weren't allowed to do. In those days we were censored—not for sex or violence in this instance but for theme. And that theme seemed to them un-American in some way."

BELOW LEFT: Johnny and the Black Rebels. More than any other, this is the film of Brando's that cemented his appeal with youthful audiences. Misunderstood, alienated and pouty, Johnny and his fellow gang members confronted not only the sleepy sensibilities of a small comfortable town but, symbolically, the constrained attitudes and mores of middle-age, middle-class America.

It was soon "cool" for kids who felt like outsiders, as Johnny and his boys did, to don jeans and leather jackets and "hang out," adopting a tough but—thankfully—usually benign attitude. Brando became a cult figure thanks to *The Wild One*, but like Stanley Kramer he was not satisfied with the outcome of the picture: "We started out to do something worthwhile, to explain the psychology of the hipster. But somewhere along the way we went off the track. The result was that instead of finding why young people tend to bunch in groups that seek expression in violence, all that we did was show the violence."

In fact, the violent theme of *The Wild One* horrified conservative segments of the moviegoing public and it was roundly denounced by various religious groups. The film was banned entirely in Britain until 1968—oddly, just prior to the release of *Easy Rider*. Marlon's reviews for *The Wild One* were more consistent than those for the film overall. The New York *Daily News* remarked, "Brando's performance is astonishing. He talks in grunts and jerks. He gives the complete picture of a worried youth needing the false security of gang violence."

ABOVE: A mock baseball game between Marlon and *Wild One* costars Yvonne Doughty and Gil Stratton. By the time of the picture's release, Brando was back in New York with Movita in tow. They were strictly, at this time, on-again, off-again, but Marlon had agreed to let her stay in his Manhattan apartment while he took a cruise to Europe. The trip was canceled, though, when he suddenly decided to return to the stage.

For three months he starred in a low-budget production of George Bernard Shaw's *Arms and the Man* presented in Long Island, Massachusetts and Connecticut. The tour was a resounding financial success—and a critical flop. Marlon was accused of walking through several performances, which he later admitted was true. He had essentially taken the job as a means to guarantee roles in the company for several of his Actors Studio cronies.

Following the Shaw tour, Brando did set sail for Europe, sans Movita as planned. He returned to Hollywood six months later to star in arguably his greatest film, *On the Waterfront*.

III

Going Hollywood

1954–1955

OPPOSITE: Brando in character for Terry Malloy, the slow-witted ex-boxer who rises to heroism in *On the Waterfront*. Based on a series of Pulitzer Prize-winning articles, the *Waterfront* screenplay by Budd Schulberg traces Malloy's struggle against the insidious corruption of the New York dockworker's union, for which he has been used as an innocent pawn in a murder. He is encouraged in his fight against a crooked union boss (Lee J. Cobb) by a local priest (Karl Malden) and by the young sister (Eva Marie Saint) of the man Malloy has unknowingly allowed to be killed. Terry does not, however, receive support from his weaselly brother Charlie (Rod Steiger), who is one of Cobb's henchmen.

Elia Kazan agreed to direct the picture for Columbia and immediately suggested Brando for the Malloy role. There was some discussion at the time about Frank Sinatra being cast but, although Sinatra begged Columbia head Harry Cohn for the part, Marlon was chosen. Sinatra never forgave Brando for winning the role and his resentment toward Marlon resurfaced two years later when *Guys and Dolls* went into production.

ABOVE: Marlon Sr. and Dorothy Brando pose with their son on the Hoboken location site for *On the Waterfront*. Through psychiatric analysis, Marlon had come to better understand his relationship with his parents. Although he and his father never really grew close, they did respect one another and later formed a production company together. Brando did, however, feel a strong attachment to his mother at this time, as she was in failing health. She would, in fact, be dead by April 1954, just four months after this visit.

Following her death, Brando told Clifford Odets that he was grateful to have come to terms with his love for Dorothy, as it was "just in time. Mother got sick and she was in the hospital. She got bad and began to die. But she told the doctors, 'I won't die until I can hold my son's hand.' Somehow she managed to stay alive until I got there—and then she held my hand and she died."

ABOVE: Brando's Terry Malloy is recognized as one of the greatest American screen characterizations. With consummate skill, he creates an inarticulate Everyman who, once awakened to the evil surrounding him, is compelled to fight for truth, even when his life is threatened. In the hands of a lesser actor, Malloy might have registered strictly as a loser, blundering through a dangerous situation. But Marlon infuses this potentially pathetic man with a surprising dignity and childlike sensitivity. The latter is most apparent in the scenes of Terry caring for his pet pigeons in their rooftop cage and in tender moments with Eva Marie Saint.

Waterfront's most famous scene—and the one by which Brando will probably be best-remembered—takes place in the backseat of a taxi. Terry is being warned by his unloyal brother Charlie to stop his crusade against the union kingpin. Terry bitterly reminds Charlie that even when they were in the fight game together he worked against Terry's interests by forcing Terry to purposely lose fights to win quick small-time bets. Charlie responds that they made good money. "Oh, Charlie," Terry tells him. "You don't understand. I coulda had class. I coulda been a contender. I coulda *been* somebody, instead of a bum—which is what I am."

Even after years of abuse at the hands of Brando impersonators, this scene is heartbreaking to watch. Pauline Kael wrote of Brando's playing of it: "He spoke for all our failed hopes. It was the great American lament." Rod Steiger, however, does not recall this immortal screen moment with fondness. In a breach of acting etiquette he has never explained, Brando left the set following his close-ups, leaving Steiger to play his important reaction shots to a stand-in. Despite this, Steiger won a "Best Supporting Actor" Oscar nomination for this work.

ABOVE: Marlon and Eva Marie Saint snuggle during a break in filming. *Waterfront* was Saint's first film and she found working with Brando a unique experience. "Marlon had an incredible sensitivity to everything around him," she recalled to writer Bob Thomas. "He was like an open wound, but what he was never got in the way of the role he had to play. It became such a natural part of him that he didn't have to put it on. When you work with other actors, something happens in their eyes as they start to assume their characters. Their eyes grow gray and glassy, the way a snake looks just before it is going to shed its skin. Actors *start acting.* But Marlon never did. He *was* Terry Malloy."

On the Waterfront opened to adulatory reviews and huge box office grosses. When Academy Award nominations were announced in February 1955, the film received eleven nods in ten categories. Brando was the recipient of his fourth "Best Actor" nomination in a row and in spite of his sometimes uncomfortable position within the Hollywood Establishment, he was the odds-on favorite to win the award. In a classic "good news/bad news" twist, Marlon received word of his nomination at his New York apartment just moments before he was served with a summons from 20th Century-Fox for a breach of contract suit in the amount of $2 million. The suit was filed because Brando had backed out of a deal with studio head Darryl F. Zanuck to star in a biblical epic entitled *The Egyptian.*

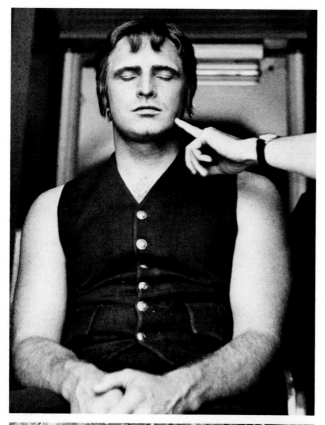

ABOVE: To resolve the Fox lawsuit, Marlon agreed to star for the studio in the romantic melodrama *Désirée*, in which he would play Napoleon. The Fox makeup department created a Bonaparte-like look for Brando by building up his nose and eyebrows and fitting him with an appropriate wig.

Marlon met the challenge of playing one of history's most famous men with only halfhearted enthusiasm. He didn't like the *Désirée* script and when asked on the set one day how he was approaching his role he quipped, "Most of the time I just let the makeup play the part."

This was the first film Brando starred in for which he didn't feel a personal connection of some kind. He had been forced into it to avoid litigation and his lack of commitment was reflected in his performance.

BELOW: Jean Simmons, in the title role, and Marlon pose for a typical publicity portrait. Under the direction of Henry Koster, *Désirée* emerged as a muddled soap opera about the rise and fall of Napoleon as seen through the eyes of Désirée, his first love. Merle Oberon costarred as his long-suffering wife Josephine.

Brando got along well with the cast and crew of *Désirée* and he felt especially relaxed with Simmons, who, like himself, recognized that the picture was nothing more than contrived pseudohistorical hokum.

ABOVE: Marlon takes a call on the set from Rita Moreno. Although Brando was still seeing Movita on a semiregular basis (and also dating actresses Susan Cabot and Pier Angeli), Moreno was his serious passion at this time. From his earliest days in New York, Marlon's attraction to dark, exotic, usually foreign women was well-known. The only blonde he seems to have romanced during his stage career was the then-svelte Shelley Winters.

Brando's affair with Moreno continued, sporadic and stormy, for several years and ended unhappily in 1961 when Rita overdosed on sleeping pills at Marlon's home. He wasn't there at the time, but luckily Moreno was discovered by a neighbor. She was rushed to a hospital and recovered. Later Moreno and Marlon settled into a comfortable friendship.

BELOW: Marlon strikes the stereotypical Napoleonic pose in a publicity still for *Désirée*. Released in late 1954, this film was not well-received by critics ("It's strictly Brando playing dress-up as Napoleon," wrote one) and it disappointed discriminating fans. Following his remarkable work in *On the Waterfront*, Marlon's unsatisfying impersonation of Napoleon came as an unwelcome surprise. *Désirée* did turn a respectable profit, thanks to the drawing power of its stars and a passion American audiences were feeling at the time for historical dramas.

OPPOSITE: During the final weeks of *Désirée* filming and a lull in his affair with Rita Moreno, Marlon met a precocious nineteen-year-old French girl who became his most publicized romance to date. Josiane Mariani-Berenger—seen here with Marlon in her native village of Bandol, France—had met Brando in New York, first at his psychiatrist's office and later at a party for Stella Adler. Josiane later told reporters that after talking with her for just two hours, Marlon proposed marriage. She accompanied him back to Hollywood for some last-minute shooting on *Désirée*, following which the couple traveled to Paris and then Bandol, where Josiane's father announced on November 1, 1954, that his daughter and Brando were engaged to be married.

Although not expecting the engagement to be announced so quickly, Brando addressed a small army of reporters gathered near Josiane's home: "I consider myself engaged to this lovely girl and I gave her an engagement ring. I wanted to make it official . . . she is a shy girl and not used to having her innermost feelings exposed to everyone." Neither was Marlon and he resented the intrusion of the world press during this whirlwind love affair—especially since he wasn't really sure if he was headed toward matrimony.

ABOVE RIGHT: Marlon departs from Paris and cheerfully declares that he will wed Josiane "within a year." Some comment was made about his business-like attire.

BELOW RIGHT: In France, Josiane poses with a photo of her intended. The genuine article was in New York, remaining adamant—publicly, at least—about his plans to marry. Josiane told the press, "I love him and he loves me and there is nothing else."

When Marlon returned to Hollywood, Josiane joined him, hoping not only to become Mrs. Brando but also to establish a career in films. She declared that her idol was Leslie Caron. After a short while, however, Brando and Josiane drifted apart and she returned to France—still single. Marlon admitted years later that he held to the engagement story in large part because the whole affair had become so public. He vowed never again to have his private life paraded through the world's headlines. "I don't want to spread the peanut butter of my personality on the moldy bread of the commercial press," he once remarked.

OPPOSITE: Jean Simmons and Marlon are reunited on the soundstages of Samuel Goldwyn's studio in a dance rehearsal for the "If I Were a Bell" number from *Guys and Dolls.* Goldwyn scooped the rights to *Guys and Dolls* out from under the nose of MGM's Dore Schary and he planned to spare no expense to make it a blockbuster.

The show, based on characters created by Damon Runyon, with music and lyrics by Frank Loesser, had been a huge Broadway hit since opening in 1951. The story concerns a colorful batch of Times Square characters and their various problems with love and gambling. Eyebrows were raised when Goldwyn offered Brando the role of Sky Masterson, the show's singing romantic lead. But Marlon was thrilled with the prospect of trying something removed from the heavy dramatics he had specialized in. Upon signing for the film, he made one of his typical off-center statements to the press: "I got tired of those intense pictures where I had to beat people over the head with a crocodile, yelling and screaming all the time."

Brando joined an interesting cast that included Simmons as his love interest Sarah Brown, an initially prim Salvation Army type; Vivian Blaine, recreating her Broadway triumph as the whining chorine Adelaide; and Frank Sinatra as Nathan Detroit, Masterson's gambling rival.

ABOVE: Marlon's vocal coach is bending behind him, giving the impression of a three-armed Brando during this song rehearsal. As with most "serious" actors, Marlon yearned to sing and dance, although he wasn't sure that he was up to the vocal demands of the *Guys and Dolls* score. He drew confidence from Joseph Mankiewicz, who signed to direct the picture. He wired Brando: UNDERSTAND YOU'RE APPREHENSIVE BECAUSE YOU'VE NEVER DONE A MUSICAL COMEDY. YOU HAVE NOTHING TO WORRY ABOUT BECAUSE NEITHER HAVE I.

Marlon told columnist Joe Hyams, "A song and dance is part of an actor's trade: he should be able to dance a jig or tell a joke as part of his bag of tricks. I've always played lugubrious, heavy things and neglected this side of the entertainment business too long." In private, Brando admitted that he was terrified about looking like an idiot in *Guys and Dolls,* particularly since he would be sharing the screen with musical veteran Sinatra.

ABOVE: The stars of *Guys and Dolls.* This is one of the few times Brando and Sinatra were caught smiling at the same time. It was no secret that Sinatra still held resentment toward Marlon for being so successful in *On the Waterfront.* Added to this was the fact that Sinatra felt *he* should have been cast as Sky Masterson, who gets to sing the lovely "I'll Know" and "Luck Be a Lady," a snappy Sinatraesque showstopper.

Once production began, Brando realized that his vocal prowess needed help. When he met Sinatra for the first time, he said, "You know, Frank, I'm new at this musical racket. So I'd appreciate it if you'd rehearse with me beforehand. I'll come to your dressing room, meet you in the rehearsal hall, anywhere you say." Sinatra responded icily. "Look, Brando," he snarled, "don't give me that Method actor shit." Things did not improve between the two stars and by the end of filming they were barely speaking to each other.

ABOVE RIGHT: In the midst of filming *Guys and Dolls,* Brando attends a dinner in honor of 1954's Oscar nominees. He is chatting here with Judy Garland, a "Best Actress" contender for *A Star Is Born,* and Edmond O'Brien, nominated for *The Barefoot Contessa.*

BELOW RIGHT: Backstage at the 1955 Academy Award ceremonies, Brando poses with his Oscar and Bette Davis, who had presented him the statuette just moments earlier for his performance in *On the Waterfront,* which was voted "Best Picture." Hollywood's rebel looked elegant in a tuxedo and he delivered a short acceptance speech. "Thank you very much," he mumbled shyly. "Uh, it's much heavier than I imagined. Uh, I, uh, I had something to say and uh, I can't remember what I, uh, was going to say for the life of me. I don't think that, uh, ever in my life have so many people been so directly responsible for my being so very, very glad. It's a wonderful moment and a rare one and I am certainly indebted. Thank you."

ABOVE: Marlon the "Method Mumbler" had come a long way since his first days as a film actor when he was sleeping on his aunt's couch in Eagle Rock. On this glamorous Oscar night, he camped it up with no less a symbol of the Hollywood Establishment than Bob Hope and even spent over an hour in the pressroom, answering questions from a battery of newspeople from all over the world.

It would be an entirely different story eighteen years later when Brando was, once again, an Oscar recipient.

ABOVE RIGHT: Back on the Goldwyn lot to resume filming *Guys and Dolls* the morning following his Oscar win, Marlon reads through a pile of congratulatory telegrams. He told reporters that his Academy Award was "safe at home" and claimed that his award-winning performance in *Waterfront* was not artfully planned in advance. "Ten minutes before we started shooting in New York on that picture," he said, "I turned to my stand-in and said, 'I've got to find a characterization.' Ten minutes to figure out a way to play a part that won an Oscar! I didn't know if I was Mutt or Jeff or Falstaff."

BELOW RIGHT: When *Guys and Dolls* opened in the fall of 1955, critics had reservations about the film generally, but were mostly kind to Marlon's performance as the slick Sky Masterson. As he feared, his unexciting singing style received some knocks. *The New Yorker* said, [He] "sings through a rather unyielding set of sinuses." Seen today, Brando's work in the film is especially appealing because it's so unlike anything he did before or since. He looks dapper and handsome and his interplay with Jean Simmons is sexy and funny.

To persuade Marlon to attend the New York and Hollywood openings of *Guys and Dolls*, Samuel Goldwyn gave him a Thunderbird convertible—then the hottest new sports car in America. Brando loved the car, but the public was less enthusiastic about the film. Despite its built-in reputation as a Broadway smash, *Guys and Dolls* performed poorly at the box office. Goldwyn was disappointed by the picture's reception, but he was proud to have produced a film with Brando, whom he called—with typical hyperbole—"the greatest actor who ever lived."

ABOVE: Hollywood's latest Oscar winner addresses an acting class on the Universal Studios lot. Clustered near Brando are (clockwise) David Janssen, John Saxon, Mamie Van Doren and Clint Eastwood. To the extreme right are seated Barbara Rush (holding cup) and Gia Scala.

Marlon always claimed that he derived little pleasure from his acting talent and he was usually loathe to discuss his "technique." But he was now considered the most influential actor in the business and he would occasionally offer a nugget or two about his approach to his craft. "An actor is at most a poet," he said, "and at least an entertainer. You can't be a poet by really trying hard. It's like being charming. You can't be charming by working at it. Also, if an actor holds back 20 percent, he'll always be honest with his audience. Try to show more than you've got to give and they catch on right away."

OPPOSITE: In a surprising move, Marlon agreed to appear on Edward R. Murrow's highly rated TV interview program "Person to Person" on April 2, 1955. Broadcast from the small Hollywood Hills bungalow Marlon had been renting for over a year, the show featured an impromptu conga drum concert and Brando's reflections on his overblown image as a kook. "I'm sick to death of having people come up to me and say hello," he told Murrow, "and then just stand there expecting me to throw a raccoon at them." Marlon would not submit to another television interview for many years.

ABOVE: Marlon was more publicly visible in 1955 than at any other time in his career. He basked in his position as Hollywood's top actor and he was more readily accessible than he would ever be again. As the year came to a close, he attended this party in New York, where he was interviewed for a radio show while Marilyn Monroe and Sid Caesar looked on. Later Monroe and Brando were seen dancing together and naturally rumors of a romance spread quickly.

Marilyn did admit to the press that she considered Marlon to be "one of the most attractive men I've ever met" and that she wanted to play opposite him in something "serious." Always discreet about his relationships with women, Brando never said much about Monroe for public consumption, but there are many who believe he and Marilyn did indeed have a brief affair at this time.

OPPOSITE: Brando was now at the very peak of his profession. The public found him a fascinating combination of tremendous talent and flagrant sex appeal; critics who had earlier derided him now hailed him as an artist of stature. He had even learned to handle the press with more finesse. His rebel image had mellowed somewhat—though not enough to render him "Establishment"—and his future success in Hollywood seemed limitless.

Unfortunately, as Marlon's stardom became secure, his films deteriorated in quality. For the next few years, he would attempt a broader range of roles; sometimes succeeding, sometimes not. He would never again, however, enjoy as consistent a period of popularity as his first five years in Hollywood had provided.

IV

Experiments
1956–1962

OPPOSITE: In March 1956 Marlon Brando Sr. and Marlon Jr. announced the formation of their independent filmmaking company, Pennebaker Productions—named in honor of Marlon's late mother. In partnership with director George Englund, father and son planned to produce pictures that would be informative and socially relevant as well as entertaining.

Pennebaker planned its first Brando vehicle to be based on stories about outreach programs sponsored by the United Nations. A scriptwriter was assigned and a fact-finding mission to Indonesia took place, but for various reasons the project never materialized. Pennebaker was not able to put together a successful Brando deal until 1958.

In the meantime, Marlon signed with MGM to play one of his most unusual roles in the screen version of the popular Broadway play *The Teahouse of the August Moon.*

ABOVE: April 11, 1956—Brando is besieged by reporters and photographers as he arrives in Tokyo to begin location filming on *The Teahouse of the August Moon.* Always attracted to the philosophies and arts of the Far East, Marlon was delighted to be shooting a picture in Japan and his stay there was illuminating. He told the press, "Americans don't even begin to understand the people of Asia. Our understanding of Asians will never improve until we get out of the habit of thinking of the people as short, spindly-legged, buck-toothed little people with strange customs."

ABOVE: Looking over the *Teahouse* script are Marlon and costars Machiko Kyo and Glenn Ford. A bittersweet comedy that pleads gently for tolerance and understanding, *Teahouse* concerns a rowdy group of American Army officers, led by Captain Frisby (Ford) and stationed near Okinawa, who come to appreciate local traditions through the comic badgering of Sakini, a "genial, foxy Okinawan interpreter," played by Brando.

Marlon had seen *Teahouse* several times during its Broadway run—with David Wayne playing Sakini—and he approached MGM about buying the play for him. The studio was pleased to do so, even when Brando announced it was Sakini he yearned to play, rather than Captain Frisby, the romantic lead. Studio head Dore Schary said, "If Marlon had wanted to play Little Eva, I would have let him."

OPPOSITE: As Sakini, Brando was required to wear a complicated, bizarre makeup that was only half-convincing on-screen. An uncomfortable rubber lid was built around Marlon's eyes, his cheekbones were accentuated with a dark cosmetic base and his eyebrows were darkened and thickened. The final touch was the addition of buckteeth and an unkempt black wig. It was a surprisingly stereotypical appearance for a man who believed so strongly in breaking down racial clichés.

ABOVE: The *Teahouse* company was not a happy one. The two stars, with their divergent backgrounds (Ford was a by-the-book product of the studio system), did not relate easily to one another. Ford resented the constant attention paid to Brando by fans and visiting reporters; Marlon didn't understand his costar's unwillingness to occasionally improvise dialogue or vary his performance.

The production was forced into two weeks of retakes when supporting actor Louis Calhern died suddenly. (He was replaced by Paul Ford.) When a month of torrential rains hit the Japanese location, MGM called the picture back to their Culver City lot for completion. By the end of filming, everyone involved in the production was thrilled to be rid of it.

The Teahouse of the August Moon opened in November 1956 to good business and reviews that praised Brando's courage in taking a role so alien to his established image. It was agreed, however, that the delicate charm of the stage version had not translated fully to the screen and that Marlon's characterization was amusing but lacked shading. After seeing the picture for the first time, Brando commented, "It's a shame. I hoped that at least some of the magic of the play would have come across on-screen." The most positive result of the *Teahouse* experience was Marlon's fascination with the Orient. He vowed to return as soon as possible. Coincidentally, his next film, *Sayonara,* allowed him to do precisely that.

OPPOSITE: On his way back to Japan for *Sayonara* location filming, Brando stopped over in London and posed for this striking portrait by Cecil Beaton. With his own Pennebaker Productions unable to come up with a suitable vehicle, Marlon agreed to star in *Sayonara* for Warner Brothers at a salary of $300,000 plus a percentage of the film's gross. It was a shrewd business decision that eventually netted Brando a small fortune.

Prior to leaving for Japan, Marlon began a romance with a beautiful exotic young Indian actress, Anna Kashfi. He first spotted her on the Paramount lot and inquired of his companion, "Who is that good-looking broad in the red sari?"

Although Brando was still seeing both Rita Moreno and Movita, he began courting Kashfi by mail from Japan.

ABOVE LEFT: Director Joshua Logan, Brando and producer William Goetz chat in the midst of filming. Based on James Michener's popular novel, *Sayonara* tells of the American Armed Forces' bigoted (and official) stand on interracial marriages between enlisted men stationed in Japan and local women during the final days of the Korean War—and how two couples are affected by this attitude.

Brando and Red Buttons were cast as soldiers who fall in love with Japanese girls and then encounter extreme hostility when they announce plans to marry the girls and return to the United States. When Buttons and his new bride (Miyoshi Umeki) collapse under the pressure and commit suicide, Brando vows to wed his lover (played by elegant newcomer Miiko Taka) and bring her back to the States in spite of the uncertain future they may face in their "mixed marriage."

BELOW LEFT: Red Buttons and Marlon enjoy a laugh on the *Sayonara* set. Today Buttons remembers his experience on this film—his first—with warmth and admiring words for his costar: "Marlon loved to clown. I used to love to make him laugh and see him smile; he has a *wonderful* smile. We got along great, just great."

Buttons and Miyoshi Umeki won "Best Supporting Actor" and "Best Supporting Actress" Oscars for their work in *Sayonara*. "I've always said this," recalls Buttons, "and I'll say it again. I think Brando's performance handed me my Oscar on a platter. When he walked in and saw both of us dead, that heart-wrenching scene that he did . . . just with saying 'Oh my God,' those three little words, he put an Oscar in my hands and in Miyoshi's hands too."

ABOVE RIGHT: "They kill me," Brando remarked to a visiting journalist. "They really kill me. Don't you think they're wonderful? Don't you love them—the Japanese kids?"

The feeling was apparently mutual, as Marlon was followed around *Sayonara* locations by children and adults alike. He captivated his female fans, who giggled nervously whenever he appeared.

BELOW RIGHT: Miiko Taka and Marlon as the lovers in *Sayonara.* "There's a lot of hearts and flowers and soft violins in it," Brando said of the picture upon its release in 1957. "But beneath the romance it attacks the prejudices that exist on the part of the Japanese, as well as on our part."

Marlon received an Academy Award nomination for his performance in *Sayonara,* but he lost the Oscar to Alec Guinness. Some critics attacked him for accepting a role that personified the Hollywood image of a romantic hero, but audiences loved him in *Sayonara* and they made the film one of the year's top moneymakers. The film would stand, in fact, as Brando's most successful until the release of *The Godfather* fifteen years later.

OPPOSITE: Brando was again in military costume, though of a decidedly different stripe, for his next film, *The Young Lions.* Under Edward Dmytryk's direction for 20th Century-Fox, he played Christian Diestl, an idealistic young Nazi whose experiences during World War II ultimately leave him filled with loathing for his country and himself.

Derived from a novel by Irwin Shaw, *The Young Lions* examines the motives of both Germany and America, as reflected in the lives of three soldiers. Besides Brando, there are two Americans: an entertainer (Dean Martin) who tries everything to avoid actual combat and a young Jew (played by Montgomery Clift) who suffers through persecution at the hands of his fellow GIs.

The Young Lions was shot partially in France. Brando took advantage of his stay in Paris to meet with Irwin Shaw and discuss the script. French journalists were impressed when Marlon publicly scolded Shaw for refusing to allow Diestl to be depicted with sympathy. "If we continue to say that all Germans are bad," he reportedly told Shaw, "we would add to the Nazi's argument that all *Jews* are bad."

ABOVE: A cigarette break with Dean Martin and Brando on location for *The Young Lions.* Surprisingly, Marlon preferred the freewheeling company of Martin over that of Montgomery Clift. A decade earlier, Brando and Clift were considered *the* most important young actors on the New York stage. Clift found success in Hollywood prior to Marlon, but his career was now beginning its tragic decline, primarily because of his deteriorating mental health. Though they were often mentioned in the same breath by writers and admirers, Brando and Clift had little in common and they were not friends. They had no scenes together in *The Young Lions* and they spoke only occasionally on the set. This contact ended entirely after Marlon suggested to Clift one afternoon that he seek psychiatric help.

One day while Brando and Martin were lunching in Paris at the Hôtel Prince de Galles, a nervous waitress spilled a pot of boiling-hot tea in Marlon's lap. The painful mishap sent him to a local hospital for two days where, he claimed, every nurse in the place turned up each time the bandage on his groin needed changing.

When Brando was asked about the incident by United Press International, he gave them a headline they would have loved to use: BRANDO SCALDS BALLS AT PRINCE DE GALLES.

71

ABOVE LEFT: When Marlon returned to Hollywood to shoot interiors for *The Young Lions*, he resumed his affair with Anna Kashfi. When she announced in the fall of 1957 that she was pregnant, Brando proposed marriage.

With his hair still blond for *Young Lions* filming, Marlon married Anna on October 11, 1957, at his Aunt Betty's Eagle Rock home. The ceremony was essentially private, with only this one photograph released to the press. There was no honeymoon. The bride and groom spent the hours after their wedding driving aimlessly around Los Angeles before settling into Brando's rented house.

Things went sour in the marriage almost from the onset. Kashfi later complained in her book about Marlon, *Brando for Breakfast*, that her new husband lacked finesse and patience when it came to lovemaking. During one apparently rough evening, she "asked if he had rape in mind. He answered, 'Rape is just assault with a friendly weapon.'"

Brando, too, had complaints. He discovered that although she had been born in Calcutta, Anna was not Indian as she had claimed. She was instead the daughter of two Londoners and her real name was Joanne O'Callaghan. Marlon felt betrayed and used and he was soon confiding to friends that the marriage had been a mistake. The birth of Marlon and Anna's son on May 11, 1958, did nothing to bring his parents together and they separated six months later. Brando named his child Christian, after the controversial character he played in *The Young Lions*.

BELOW LEFT: *The Young Lions* opened in the fall of 1958 to good reviews. *Time* said of Marlon's performance: "Brando underplays to the point where in many a scene only a telepathist could hope to tell what he is thinking; but in the long run he imparts an urgent and moving sense that there is a soul somewhere inside the lieutenant's uniform."

The lure of the picture's three stars proved to be potent at the box office. *The Young Lions* was, in fact, the last of Brando's films for many years to turn a healthy profit.

ABOVE: Early in 1959 Brando began one of the most unique projects of his career—directing himself in *One-Eyed Jacks*. After four years in business, Pennebaker Productions had finally came up with a suitable script for Marlon. Taken from Charles Neider's novel *The Authentic Death of Hendry Jones, One-Eyed Jacks* is a tale of revenge set in 1885 Mexico. Brando is Rio the Kid, a young bank robber who is betrayed by his older partner, Dad Longworth, played by Karl Malden. Longworth allows the Kid to be captured and sent to prison for five years, during which time Longworth becomes the respectable sheriff of a small village. When Rio is released, he tracks Longworth down, seduces his young stepdaughter and eventually kills him.

A simple enough story of Western vengeance, *One-Eyed Jacks* took on near-mythic proportions because of the behind-the-scenes struggle to get it made. The first script by Sam Peckinpah was discarded and Calder Willingham was called in for a rewrite. Stanley Kubrik was originally signed to direct, but he and Brando failed to agree on much of anything and he was dismissed four weeks prior to filming. Calder Willingham also left the production at the last minute and in the midst of this confusion Marlon decided to direct the picture himself. Paramount, who held the releasing deal for the film, had no objection, as long as Brando could get the film made for the $1.8 million allotted for the budget.

ABOVE LEFT: Brando shows Karl Malden how he wants a scene to be played between Malden and his young stepdaughter. Malden had been a friend and occasional costar of Marlon's since working with him in *Truckline Cafe* and he was enthusiastic about Brando's talents as a director. "There is this impact and unity about Marlon as an actor; I think he may have brought it to his first directorial job," Malden said on the *One-Eyed Jacks* set. "He has taken the classic folk form of the outdoor Western drama and approached it with honesty and truth. On the practical level, Brando the director is patient, determined and intelligent."

BELOW LEFT: Marlon offers an interesting pose for Paramount's still photographer on the *One-Eyed Jacks* location near Monterey, California. The production schedule on the film had stretched from two months to six and word was filtering back to Hollywood that Brando was overrehearsing, overshooting and *way* over budget. He insisted on taking an entire day to capture a moment that would last only three seconds on screen and at one point he insisted that he and Malden get drunk to better play a drunk scene. After they staggered through several takes, it was decided to shoot the scene when the actors were sober, but in the meantime hundreds of feet of film had been wasted.

Paramount watched in horror as the *Jacks* budget escalated to $6 million, with Brando demanding retakes on several key scenes. "This isn't a film," cracked producer Frank Rosenberg, "it's a way of life." Brando completed the picture in June 1959, at which time it was noted that he had set a new world's record by exposing over one million feet of film stock. His first cut of the picture ran close to five hours in length.

OPPOSITE: After Paramount trimmed the picture down to two hours and twenty minutes (and reshot the ending months after the production had shut down), *One-Eyed Jacks* debuted in March 1961— over two years after it began filming. Reviews were mixed, but public reaction was positive. The picture reportedly earned $12 million upon its initial release, but because of its costs was considered only a partial success.

Marlon was disappointed in the final print. "Now, it's a good picture for them [Paramount]," he said upon its release, "but it's not the picture I made . . . now the characters in the film are black-and-white, not gray-and-human as I planned them."

Seen today, Brando's only directorial effort remains as mercurial as the man behind it. The description of *One-Eyed Jacks* offered by Brando biographer Tony Thomas is apt: "[It] is uneven in its storytelling, probably due to the severe editing, but it also has a dichotomy of directional style. On the one hand it is tough and realistic and on the other it is softly romantic. The picture has excitement and violence, but it is also moody, sensuous and occasionally sadomasochistic."

ABOVE LEFT: Brando and Anna Kashfi ignore each other as they pass enroute to a court hearing in Santa Monica, California, in October 1959. Marlon was claiming that Anna had not complied with the child visitation rights agreement of their divorce action filed the previous April. Later court battles between Marlon and Anna would prove to be headline-grabbers.

BELOW LEFT: Following his separation from Kashfi, Marlon again dated several exotic starlets, including Barbara Luna and France Nuyen—seen with him here in a Japanese restaurant. Hollywood gossips assumed that Rita Moreno and Movita were out of Brando's romantic life. It was common knowledge that he had spent weekends away from the filming of *One-Eyed Jacks* visiting France Nuyen in New York. When asked by reporters if he would be marrying Nuyen, Marlon said, "I don't think that is any of your business."

No one could have guessed, least of all Brando himself, that just a few months following this evening in Little Tokyo he would indeed be married—but not to France Nuyen.

On June 4, 1960, Marlon wed Movita in a secret ceremony in Xochimilco, Mexico. As with his first wedding, Brando's bride was pregnant. A few months later (the exact date is unavailable), Miko, Brando's second son, was born. The public remained unaware of Brando's marriage for some time.

ABOVE: Ten years after his triumph in *A Streetcar Named Desire*, Brando agreed to star in another Tennessee Williams drama, but one of greatly inferior quality. *The Fugitive Kind* placed him in the company of (from left to right) Joanne Woodward, Anna Magnani, director Sidney Lumet and cinematographer Boris Kaufman.

Taken from Williams's play *Orpheus Descending*, *The Fugitive Kind* is about an enigmatic, sexy wanderer, Val Xavier (Brando), whose conspicuous presence in a small Southern town disrupts the lives of two women: Lady Torrence (Magnani), a sexually repressed earth mother whose husband is terminally ill, and Carol (Woodward), an alcoholic young tramp.

Magnani had the film's best role and Brando knew it. For the first time in his motion picture career, he actively attempted to upstage his costar at every opportunity. Magnani in turn performed with ferocious energy—even during rehearsals. She was thrown by Marlon's habit of holding back unless the camera was rolling and she complained to Lumet that Brando's mumbled dialogue kept her from hearing her proper cues. It was a tension-filled set, with gifted actors—who should have known better—acting like insecure amateurs. Only Woodward seems to have approached the job with professionalism.

OPPOSITE: With typical filmmaking logic, *The Fugitive Kind* was shot neither in the South where its story is set, nor on a Hollywood soundstage, but in Milton, New York, a small Hudson Valley town. During a break in filming, Marlon was photographed chatting with Elizabeth Collier, a local retired English professor. According to a publicity release accompanying the photo, she and Brando "became fast friends after her visit."

When Marlon signed for this second-rate Tennessee Williams vehicle, he established a pattern that would cause him to lose respect among many of his peers and critics and all but sabotage his career in the future: he took the role strictly for the salary he was offered. Granted, it was an impressive salary; by agreeing to star in *The Fugitive Kind*, Brando became the first actor in Hollywood history to be paid $1 million for his services.

ABOVE: When *The Fugitive Kind* opened in the fall of 1961, it was greeted with harsh reviews. Most critics complained that three Oscar-winning performers (Magnani and Woodward were recent recipients of the award) should have chosen better material. Writing for *The Saturday Review,* Hollis Alpert remarked, "Watching [the film] is a painful experience. It gave me the miseries, frankly, and I state that in the past I have frequently admired practically everyone concerned with it." When asked his opinion of the picture, Tennessee Williams replied, "It's Anna Magnani's film, but Joanne Woodward is brilliant in it too. Marlon Brando," he added, "is Marlon Brando. I just wish he didn't remember Kowalski so well."

For his next film, Marlon chose to portray a character that was as far from Stanley Kowalski as one can get. After turning down an offer from producer Sam Spiegel to star in *Lawrence of Arabia*—"I'll be damned if I'll spend two years of my life out in the desert on some fucking camel!"—he chose instead to play Fletcher Christian in MGM's lavish remake of *Mutiny on the Bounty.* As it turned out, he would have been better off on the camel.

OPPOSITE: Joining Brando on the Tahitian location for *Mutiny on the Bounty* are director Carol Reed and Taritatum a Teripaiam (Tarita), a local girl who was discovered by Marlon and cast as his love interest in the picture. She would soon become his off-screen lover as well.

MGM approached the *Bounty* remake with great enthusiasm. The 1935 version, which had starred Clark Gable and Charles Laughton, was considered a classic and the studio hoped to recreate the magic of the original—this time in glorious color and with Brando following in Gable's footsteps.

From the start, however, *Bounty* proved to be a jinxed production. Carol Reed had originally been signed to direct, but he left the project after several months because of disagreements with Trevor Howard (who was playing Captain Bligh) and a small army of script doctors who were delivering rewrites hourly. The company was forced to abandon the Tahiti location because of inclement weather, tropical illness, innumerable problems with props and hassles with extras. After a period of filming at the Culver City lot, the *Bounty* crew was forced to return to Tahiti *twice* before principal photography was completed.

In response to on-set noise Brando began wearing earplugs even during filming. It was an eccentricity that infuriated some coworkers, but Marlon continued the habit on most of his future films.

ABOVE: Marlon learns a native dance during a respite from *Bounty* filming. The almost constant turmoil involved in getting this picture made was acceptable to Brando only because he fell so in love with Tahiti and its French Polynesian way of life. After the first day of shooting, Marlon turned to Carol Reed and said, "I'm sorry to see this day come; it means one day sooner that we'll be going back to the States."

For the first time since becoming a star, Brando felt completely at ease among crowds of people. Most of the islanders were unaware of his celebrity and he was able to do what he pleased without being hounded by the press or overzealous fans.

During *Bounty* production, Marlon rented a small bungalow near the Tahitian capital of Papeete, but as he spent more and more time in the area over the years—he always returned immediately after finishing a film in Hollywood—he ultimately acquired an entire island of his own, where he built a large compound which assured his privacy from curious tourists.

OPPOSITE: Brando's new tranquil life in Tahiti was rooted in his deepening relationship with Tarita. The press picked up on the romance quickly and Marlon saw no reason to keep it secret, as his marriage to Movita was still not public knowledge. In an odd coincidence only the world of movies could provide, Tarita was playing the same role opposite Brando that Movita had portrayed opposite Gable in the earlier version of *Mutiny on the Bounty.*

As with all of his personal relationships, Marlon kept the details of his affair with Tarita private. It is not known, for example, if the couple was ever legally married. They were together for many years and their first child, a boy named Tehotu, was born in 1962.

ABOVE: December 1961—Anna Kashfi takes a swing at Brando as they emerge from the Santa Monica Court. This particular battle concerned not only Marlon's visitation rights in regard to Christian, now three and a half years old, but also the issue of who would be granted full custody of the child.

During these proceedings, Marlon—wearing the ponytail hairstyle required for *Mutiny*—recalled several instances when Kashfi showed up unannounced at his Hollywood home and caused a scene. "One night," he testified, "I was awakened by the person I was with. Then I saw Anna. She had broken into my house and jumped on the bed and started pulling the girl's hair out. The girl was terrified and she beat it. Then Anna started wrecking the house." Kashfi recalled another violent quarrel during which Brando "got a knife out of the kitchen drawer, pushed it in my hands and said, 'Why don't you kill me?' I said, 'You're not worth it.' "

Added to these revelations, to Brando's dismay, was the disclosure that Marlon was secretly married to Movita and was the father of her son. Amazingly, Marlon's relationship with Tarita was never mentioned during the trial. None of this spoke well of either Kashfi or Brando as ideal parental material and the court decided that Christian would be placed temporarily in the custody of Marlon's sister Frances.

83

ABOVE: *Mutiny on the Bounty* cost MGM more than $18 million and naturally Brando was blamed for most of the budget overrun. He was chastised in a nasty *Saturday Evening Post* article, "The Mutiny of Marlon Brando," which accused him of causing virtually all of the film's problems—financial and otherwise. MGM did little to discourage this criticism—the studio was in desperate need of a scapegoat. Across town, Fox was taking a similar position with *Cleopatra*, blaming Elizabeth Taylor for all that was wrong with *that* elephantine production.

Brando filed suit against *The Saturday Evening Post* and, although the action was later dropped, *Mutiny on the Bounty* had been effectively sabotaged. The public showed scant interest in seeing a production "ruined" by the excesses of a spoiled superstar.

Marlon defended himself to writer Vernon Scott, "I'll tell you why [the film] cost so much. They started shooting without a script . . . the studio sent the entire cast and crew on location to Tahiti, where it cost them $32,000 a day—and we were out there six months all totaled! The ship cost $750,000 to build and caught fire five times. Then there was the director problem, which had nothing to do with me. The entire first three months of filming under Reed was junked for a whole new concept for [Lewis] Milestone. That cost a few dollars too."

OPPOSITE: Marlon and Movita attend the November 15, 1962, Hollywood opening of *Mutiny on the Bounty*. Although they were not living together, the Brandos put up this brief show of family unity for the sake of Marlon's custody fight with Anna Kashfi.

Mutiny on the Bounty received mixed reviews. Arthur Knight, writing for *The Saturday Review* said, "Above all it is spectacular—and spectacle, in the most literal sense, is something that must be seen." Marlon's unusual—some say daring—interpretation of Fletcher Christian was generally characterized as an acting risk that didn't quite succeed. Unlike Gable's earthy, heroic approach, Brando played Christian as an intellectual, languid dandy. *Time* said, "As Brando rather too trickily imagines him, he is a fop to his fingertips but an aristocrat to the core." *Mutiny on the Bounty* was a box office dud. It is doubtful that the anti-Brando publicity was entirely to blame, but for whatever reason the public stayed away. The picture did, however, go on to receive an Academy Award nomination as the year's best film.

ABOVE LEFT: On the set of his next film, *The Ugly American*, Marlon discusses a scene with director George Englund, one of his partners in Pennebaker Productions. By now Brando had lost interest in producing his own films—he sold Pennebaker around this time to the Musical Corporation of America (MCA) to guarantee an income for his father's remaining years.

A best-selling novel by Eugene Burdick and William J. Lederer, *The Ugly American* created controversy by suggesting that American diplomatic policies in the fictitious Asian country of Sarkhan were self-serving and detrimental to the local population. Marlon saw the film version as an opportunity to vent his pro-Asian sentiments while at the same time showing what he believed to be the arrogance and corruptibility of many American politicians.

In *The Ugly American*, Marlon played a U.S. ambassador who arrives in Sarkhan (a thinly disguised version of Thailand) just as the puppet regime established by the Americans is collapsing.

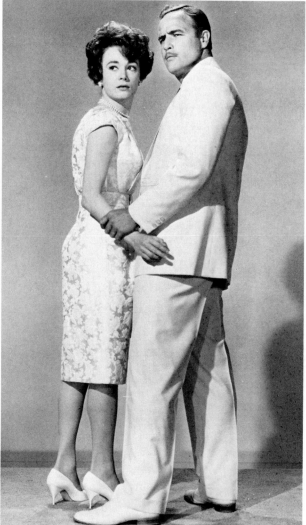

BELOW LEFT: Sandra Church played Brando's wife in *The Ugly American;* she joined him here in a typical studio pose.

To the chagrin of Universal Pictures, *The Ugly American*—thanks to the book's reputation—was perceived as un-American in some camps even as it was being filmed in Thailand. Before anyone had seen a rough print, the film was denounced in Washington by Senator William Fulbright and in Hollywood by Samuel Goldwyn. Brando defended it after returning from location filming. "There are few countries left where a picture like this could be made," he said. "It couldn't be done in France . . . certainly not in Russia. Only America, England, Sweden and a few other countries would permit such self-criticism."

While he was in Thailand, Marlon was approached by a native woman who had no idea of his identity. "What do you do for a living?" she asked. "I make faces," Brando replied.

OPPOSITE: Reaction to *The Ugly American* upon its release in late 1962 was less than enthusiastic. It was criticized not so much for its political stand as for its slow-paced dramaturgy. Marlon's performance was thoughtfully conceived but lacking in passion and the public failed to respond to the picture.

The Ugly American might have been the victim of poor timing. Had it been released five years later, at the height of the Vietnam conflict—which in a way it foretold—it would have been embraced by the antiwar sympathizers. Seen today, the picture does seem to be ahead of its time, but it still suffers from an overall dullness.

Marlon was stung by the failure of *The Ugly American;* it had been another attempt to broaden his acting image and it had not succeeded. His career was beginning a gradual descent into mediocrity that would take years to pull out of.

V

Disappointments
1963–1971

OPPOSITE: July 28, 1963—Brando takes part in a protest staged by the Congress of Racial Equality (C.O.R.E.) in the L.A. suburb of Torrance, California. The event was held because of alleged discriminating policies within a new housing development.

Although always concerned with social issues, Marlon didn't "go public" with his beliefs until 1960, when he joined Shirley MacLaine and other celebrities in a junket to California Governor Edmund G. Brown's office in Sacramento to protest the execution of convicted rapist Caryl Chessman.

Brando knew that his visible stand on controversial issues would affect his popularity (indeed, his films were all but banned in certain areas of the South after he spoke out for black rights), but he was becoming less enchanted than ever with his stardom. "What has acting given me?" he asked in 1962. "Money, notoriety, fame, fortune, success. What *about* success? It doesn't add anything to your life and, as a matter of fact, it takes a lot away. It destroys some people. Look at Marilyn Monroe. It never earned her a nickel's worth—a dime's worth —of happiness."

ABOVE: April 1963—A cheerful pose of Marlon with Harry Belafonte and James Baldwin on the steps of the Lincoln Memorial following the historic March on Washington. Shortly after this, Brando told *Ebony* magazine, "I think there are many Negroes now, just as there are many white people, who are not awakened to what is happening. Very few people understand what the nature of this movement is . . . I don't know when it began for me, but I know that the end can only be won when there is hard legislation that supports all of the issues that Reverend Martin Luther King, Reverend Ralph Abernathy, the N.A.A.C.P. and C.O.R.E. people have set down.

"These guys," he continued, "[Senator] Faubus and the rest of them, are looking for the vote. Privately, perhaps, they know that integration is inevitable. But publicly they've got to say that 'We don't want the Negroes to come here to do this and to be with us.' Otherwise, they're not going to get elected—and they want to get elected."

OPPOSITE: From the relevance of the March on Washington, Marlon segued into the nonsense of his next picture, *Bedtime Story.* In a comic-romantic role that was better-suited to the talents of Rock Hudson, Brando played a con man who, in competition with his partner David Niven, attempts to seduce wealthy women in the glamour capitals of Europe.

In a cliché-ridden plot by Stanley Shapiro, who created several Doris Day comedies, and Paul Henning, chief writer for "The Beverly Hillbillies," Brando is forced to play a lecherous, unlikable buffoon. He assumes several disguises, including that of a lunatic prince of a fictitious country (seen here), to better seduce Shirley Jones, whom he mistakenly believes is a wealthy American soap heiress.

ABOVE: Shirley Jones told this writer that the *Bedtime Story* set was a happy one and that Marlon seemed to be having "a good time." He yearned to be a proficient comedy actor and deferred to David Niven in several scenes, as he felt Niven was a master of screen farce.

Because he was slightly heavier than he had ever been, Marlon was concerned about his looks for the film, particularly since he was playing a romantic lead. "He was always worried about his makeup," remarked Jones, "and he always thought he was too fat. He was often changing the lighting or calling in the makeup man . . . he was definitely concerned. I think one of the reasons he preferred doing real character parts was because he didn't have to worry about his looks. It's funny in a way because I think he looks wonderful in *Bedtime Story.*"

Audiences responded well to the film, making it a fair-sized hit. But critics were not impressed. It was called "leering," "crass" and a "waste of time" for its cast. In the New York *Herald Tribune,* Judith Crist labeled it "a vulgar soporific for the little-brained ones."

OPPOSITE: "I need the money," Brando said in 1965 just before agreeing to star in *Morituri.* "It is like a car and a dipstick. You look at it once in a while and find that you need oil. Well, every so often I look at my financial condition and I find I need money, so I do a good-paying picture. You see, I have three households to support and I pay alimony to two women."

As directed by Bernhard Wicki for Fox, *Morituri* is a muddled, confusing espionage tale about a German pacifist (Brando) who turns out to be a Nazi saboteur aboard a cargo ship captained by Yul Brynner. Plot complications include a bloody failed mutiny and the murder of a young Jewish girl (Janet Margolin) who was selling her body to the crew of the ship.

ABOVE RIGHT: The cast of *Morituri:* Yul Brynner, Janet Margolin, Wally Cox (who had a small role) and Brando. Although pleased to be working with longtime friend Cox, Marlon was not happy during the location filming—off the coast of Catalina—for *Morituri.* He quarreled constantly with director Wicki and reportedly demanded dozens of retakes on scenes only he deemed important.

Brando told one visitor to the set, "Making this picture has been like pushing a prune pit with my nose from here to Cucamonga . . . of course if the movie is good, all the grief will be forgotten. But when a picture is bad, all you can do is stick a lampshade on your head and stand real still and hope nobody notices you."

BELOW RIGHT: An advertising montage for *Morituri,* released in the fall of 1965. This dreary film failed to find an audience and Brando was raked over the coals by critics who accused him of selling out his great career by parodying his earlier performances.

Pauline Kael, one of his biggest early boosters, said, "Like many another great actor who has become fortune's fool, he plays the great ham. He seems pleased with the lines, as if he's just thought them up. He gives the best ones a carefully timed double take so that we, too, can savor his cleverness and the delight of his German accent."

ABOVE LEFT: A slouchy, sexy pose of Marlon in costume for *The Chase*, another film that failed to live up to its potential. On paper it looked like the blockbuster Brando's career sorely needed: produced by Sam Speigel *(On the Waterfront, The Bridge on the River Kwai)*, directed by respected newcomer Arthur Penn *(The Miracle Worker)*, with a screenplay by Lillian Hellman from a book and play by Horton Foote and a cast of impressive names: Jane Fonda, Robert Redford, Angie Dickinson, Miriam Hopkins and Robert Duvall.

Marlon was cast as a sheriff of high principles who tries to keep control of his small Southern town while the locals are fired up in pursuit of an escaped convict (Redford) whom the sheriff believes to be innocent. Despite the sheriff's precautions, the convict is gunned down on the courthouse steps in a scene that brings to mind Jack Ruby's killing of Lee Harvey Oswald. Naturally, as with all Southern melodramas, *The Chase* contains its share of seamy sexual secrets as a counterpoint to the main story line.

BELOW LEFT: Costars James Fox and Jane Fonda enjoy a laugh with Brando on the set of *The Chase*. Midway through production, Marlon became convinced that the picture was being ruined because certain executives at the studio (Columbia) were insisting on too high a level of violence.

Brando protested to director Penn, but to no avail. "Fuck 'em," he said to Stanley Kramer, who visited the set. "If they're going to be so stupid, I'll just take the money, do what they want and get out. I don't give a damn about anything." It's possible that Marlon's mood was partly the result of unpleasantness in his personal life. He was still battling Anna Kashfi for full custody of their son, and in July 1965 Marlon Sr. died unexpectedly.

OPPOSITE: *The Chase* proved to be one of the major disappointments of the film year. Despite its stellar cast, the public ignored it and reviews varied from mixed to poor. In the New York *Times,* Bosley Crowther called the picture "phony and tasteless" and said of Brando's performance: "He just rides around in his prowl car. To be sure, the character assigned him is ambiguous and gross and Mr. Brando cannot make it any more than a stubborn, growling cop." Pauline Kael tagged *The Chase* a "liberal sadomasochistic fantasy."

ABOVE LEFT: Marlon is unkempt in this close-up from his next picture, *The Appaloosa.* As an "aging saddle tramp," Brando is a man obsessed with the recovery of his stolen horse, a select breed named in the film's title. Anjanette Comer plays a young woman who takes the horse in an attempt to escape the clutches of her villainous lover, portrayed by John Saxon. As this slow-moving tale of recovery and revenge is played out, the Saxon character is killed, leaving Brando and Comer to ride off together on the beloved Appaloosa.

Asked by Marlon to describe the story, John Saxon replied, "Boy meets horse, boy loses horse, boy gets horse." In an unusual occurrence, *The Appaloosa* was shot in sequence, a method of filming Brando enjoyed but seldom experienced. He did not, however, enjoy having pages of dialogue submitted to him for the first time just hours before shooting each day. "We've got no script," Marlon complained to director Sidney J. Furie when the company arrived at the St. George, Utah, location site. "Yes," replied Furie, "but when I started *Ipcress* [the director had received praise for *The Ipcress File,* released a year earlier], I had no script either. At any rate, I consider it a real privilege to be working with you." "Bullshit," Brando responded.

BELOW LEFT: A cleaned-up Brando with costar Anjanette Comer in a scene from *The Appaloosa.* Besides the script problems, Marlon grew annoyed with the director's penchant for arty camera angles and lighting. He agreed with one crew member who remarked, "Furie's shooting up the horse's ass!" This strange visual approach to the film was criticized at the time of its theatrical release and is especially grating when the picture is viewed on television.

ABOVE: *The Appaloosa* opened in October 1966 and quickly disappeared. Critics called the picture "an interesting failure" and Brando came in for his (by now) usual scolding. The Washington *Post* said, "Brando's self-indulgence over a dozen years is costing him and his public his talents."

The decline in Marlon's professional life brought forth his bitterest comments about his work. "Acting is a bum's life, in that it leads to perfect self-indulgence," he remarked. "You get paid for doing nothing and it all adds up to nothing. The last fifteen years of my life seem never to have happened; they've just gone up the chimney without any im-pression or impact on me at all . . . I still feel that Hollywood is a cultural boneyard."

Statements such as these (plus his candor about working primarily for the money) did nothing to endear Brando to producers, critics or fans. He seemed bored with his career and he was boring his admirers by being so open about his dissatisfaction and choosing such poor vehicles.

For a change, he went into his next project with enthusiasm: not for the role but for the man behind the production—the film artist he revered above all others, Charles Chaplin.

ABOVE: A candid shot of Marlon, Sophia Loren and two extras on the set of *A Countess from Hong Kong.* Charles Chaplin came out of a lengthy retirement to write and direct this old-fashioned romantic comedy about a destitute Russian countess (Loren) who escapes the Hong Kong police (and a phony prostitution charge) by hiding aboard a ship that is owned by an American millionaire, played by Brando. During the course of the cruise, Marlon and Sophia change from adversaries to lovers and complications arise when Brando's wife (Tippi Hedren) comes aboard unexpectedly. Naturally, Marlon and Sophia are united at the film's end.

Based on a story he had originally written in 1931, Chaplin completed a screenplay for *Countess* in 1965 and announced that he would make the film only on the condition that Loren and Brando play the leads. Sophia Loren, then at the peak of her popularity, was flattered by the compliment and signed for the picture immediately.

Brando was not so sure about the film. He flew to London to discuss it and was completely charmed by Chaplin, who acted out the entire script for Marlon in his hotel suite. Signing for the picture, Brando said he had accepted "because Chaplin asked me. When a man of his stature in the industry writes a script for you, you can hardly refuse." Marlon did not add that he was also unable to refuse the $1-million-plus salary he would be getting.

ABOVE: As *A Countess from Hong Kong* got under way, it soon became obvious to both Brando and Loren that they were trapped in a production headed for certain disaster.

Chaplin (right) directed in a style derived from his silent movie days. He mimed every line of the script, every body movement, every facial expression and expected his actors to follow his "performance" to the letter. His stars were allowed no latitude whatsoever in defining their characters. There was no way Brando could practice his habit of digging for subtle facets in his role and Loren,

noted for her all-out robust style, felt equally constrained by Chaplin's technique. But both actors worshipped their director and they deferred to his every wish.

"Chaplin's a nice old gent," Brando said to a British columnist. "We do things his way, that's all. He shows us how; he doesn't really know how a scene works until he does it himself. So I've just been following directions." Marlon was upbeat publicly, but he admitted privately that Chaplin's writing and direction were hopelessly passé and that *Countess* would probably bomb.

ABOVE LEFT: The press yearned for a romance to develop between Brando and Loren, but the two sex symbols barely established a friendship. Loren was hurt when she heard that Marlon had remarked to a crew member, "Sophia isn't very feminine." And she was shocked when—during an intimate close-up—Brando said to her, "You have black hair in your nostrils."

By the end of filming, Sophia was accusing Brando of chewing garlic before shooting their love scenes.

BELOW LEFT: *Countess* production shut down for two weeks when Marlon was forced to undergo an emergency appendectomy. Prior to the operation, Brando said to the film's publicist, "If I should die, I want one thing clear: there will be no publicity photos of Sophia weeping over my grave."

It would have taken such an occurrence to generate box office success for *A Countess from Hong Kong.*

One of the most publicized, eagerly awaited pictures of the late sixties, *Countess* proved to be a crushing disappointment for fans of its stars and director. The reviews ranged from nasty to cruel. "[It's] bad enough to make a new generation of moviegoers wonder what the Chaplin cult is all about," said the London *Times.* In response to the overwhelming critical barbs, Chaplin bravely said, "I still think it's a great film," but he never worked on a picture again.

As for Marlon, his career was now in almost irreparable jeopardy—in the thirties he would have been labeled "box office poison." He was depressed to think that he had starred with one of the world's top female stars under the direction of a living legend and had come up with another failure. Unfortunately, he would soon repeat the exact same formula, with the same disappointing results.

OPPOSITE: Brando and his companion Martha Bennet are photographed in Rome, February 1967. The press speculated. Was Bennet a secretary or a new lover? Marlon, as usual, was mute on the subject. During this period, he divided his time equally between Europe, California, New York and the South Pacific. His name was linked with several women, but it seemed clear that Brando considered his home base to be with Tarita in Tahiti.

Marlon's shadowy marital status came to the fore in June of 1967 when Movita suddenly filed for divorce on the grounds of "great mental suffering." She demanded $8,000 per month alimony and child support, but in a bizarre twist Brando had his marriage to Movita annulled a year later when it was learned that she had never divorced her first husband, an "Irish crooner-boxer" named Jack Doyle.

ABOVE: Elizabeth Taylor and Marlon rehearse a scene for *Reflections in a Golden Eye*, which they began filming in Rome in the fall of 1967 under John Huston's direction.

Taken from a short story by Carson McCullers, *Reflections* is a disquieting tale about the inhabitants of an Army base in the South in 1948 and the murder that results from their various sexual problems.

Brando is Major Weldon Penderton, a withdrawn, vain career soldier who is constantly taunted about his sexual impotence by his dominating, unfaithful wife Leonora (Taylor). The

Pendertons' drab lives are disrupted by the arrival of a handsome young GI, played by Robert Forster. A latent homosexual, Penderton is drawn to the man, who in turn is obsessed with Leonora—he sneaks into her bedroom at night just to watch her sleep. The story ends with Penderton killing the GI during one of his nocturnal visits to Leonora.

Taylor had originally agreed to star in *Reflections* opposite her friend Montgomery Clift in the hope that it would revive his sinking career. When Clift died shortly before production was scheduled to begin, Brando was brought into the project as a replacement.

ABOVE RIGHT: Unlike some of his recent roles, Brando found Major Penderton a provocative challenge. He played him as a military man at war with his suppressed emotions and, as with all of his best performances, it was the subtleties he chose to examine that brought the character to life.

The way he preened, almost girlishly, in the mirror before morning inspection, the flat monotone—drained of all spirit—he used when talking with his wife, the childlike way he fondled a spoon he had stolen from a fellow officer he was attracted to contributed to a courageous performance that made 1967 audiences squirm.

Production of *Reflections in a Golden Eye* went smoothly. Marlon got on well with Taylor and Huston and the only difficulty occurred offscreen. Tarita visited Brando during filming, bringing their son Tehotu with her. The local *paparazzi* set up a round-the-clock vigil outside Marlon's rented home on the island of Tiberia in the hope of getting a shot of the family together. When one photographer approached Tarita and the child unexpectedly, Brando slugged him. He also reportedly threatened the other photographers with a broken bottle.

BELOW RIGHT: Brando's fascinating performance in *Reflection in a Golden Eye* was not appreciated when the film opened. It made most critics uncomfortable, but has become more appreciated with the passage of twenty years. The film, too, has developed a minor cult following, as much for its seamy story as for its high-powered cast. But it was not successful when originally released. Audiences had difficulty relating to or sympathizing with the characters and the genre of Southern-based sexual melodramas was out of style.

Reflections added little luster to the reputations of Brando and Huston and its failure marked the beginning of Elizabeth Taylor's fall from the top of the box office lists.

ABOVE: Just weeks after the assassination of Martin Luther King touched off bloody rioting in the area, Brando joined New York Mayor John Lindsay on a "goodwill stroll" through Harlem in May 1968.

"I believe with the late Martin Luther King that we are either going to learn to live together as brothers in this country or die separately as fools," Marlon told reporters.

ABOVE: A month later, there were no smiles when Marlon attended a memorial service for a slain Black Panther member in Berkeley, California. "It is either nonviolence or nonexistence," he said after the service. "I have three children and I would not like to think that they will grow up in a world filled with strife."

Press reports at this time claimed that Brando was so devastated by the death of Reverend King—and Robert F. Kennedy—that he would be retiring from films to devote his full time to the struggle for civil rights. He did indeed make himself as available as possible for demonstrations, meetings, fund-raisers, and so on on behalf of blacks and another favorite cause, the plight of the American Indian, but realistically he couldn't have retired. His financial obligations were too demanding.

ABOVE: After turning down offers to star in *Butch Cassidy and the Sundance Kid* (in whichever role he preferred) and Elia Kazan's *The Arrangement*, Brando decided to take the role of Grindl, a bumbling guru, in the sex comedy *Candy*. He is seen here with Ewa Aulin, who played the title character.

Directed by novice Christian Marquand with a heavy hand and a nod to the drug-influenced youth market, *Candy* is the story of a young nymphet's sexual adventures told in a series of vignettes. Besides Brando's guru, she encounters Richard Burton as a besotted Welsh poet, Ringo Starr as a Mexican gardener, Walter Matthau as a blustery brigadier general and James Coburn as a brain surgeon.

The erotic charm of Terry Southern's humorous novel was completely lost in this inane, boring film version. Its blaring rock soundtrack and psychedelic-inspired camerawork did not, as planned, bring in the youthful audiences.

OPPOSITE: To many, *Candy* represents the nadir of Marlon's career. Taken on its own terms, however, Brando's performance is not at all bad; his Indian accent is funny and precise and his elaborate attempt to seduce Candy is amusing. But the film is terrible—it was savaged in reviews and did not do well financially. Critics pondered the taste of the gifted actors involved in the production.

The press was now pointing to Brando and Burton as sad examples of great talents going to waste.

ABOVE: Marlon's lengthening list of poor films was joined by *The Night of the Following Day,* which he filmed in France in 1968. He joined ex-lover Rita Moreno—here with Brando and costar Jess Hahn— in a complicated kidnapping caper. Cast as Bud (Brando's childhood nickname), Marlon played a jive-talking chauffeur who, along with Moreno as a jittery dope addict, Hahn as her moronic brother and Richard Boone as a sexual sadist, kidnaps a British teenager played by Pamela Franklin.

ABOVE RIGHT: Brando looks on as Richard Boone terrorizes Pamela Franklin in *The Night of the Following Day*. The convoluted plot of this cynical film had Franklin tortured by Boone, Moreno bedded by Brando—ostensibly to calm her down—police sneaking around disguised as fishermen, Moreno and Hahn murdered by Boone, Boone murdered by Brando and Franklin rescued.

The film ends with Franklin waking up on an airliner, glancing at stewardess Moreno and realizing it has all been a dream.

Marlon did not get along with director Hubert Cornfield and for the final weeks of shooting he had him replaced by Boone, who was an old Actors Studio chum of Brando's.

BELOW RIGHT: "Marlon Brando in his new film looks better but acts worse than I can remember for a long time," said one review of *The Night of the Following Day*, released late in 1969. Marlon did cut a trim figure in the picture, but his looks were sabotaged by an ill-fitting blond wig. The film bombed, confirming Marlon's initial reaction to the script: "It makes about as much sense to me as a rat fucking a grapefruit."

ABOVE: Brando's only 1970 release was the troubled historical drama *Burn!* (also released in some areas under the title *Queimada!*). Marlon played a British agent sent to a small Caribbean island in 1845 to break the Portuguese rule by assisting in a native uprising.

Filming began in Colombia in a jungle area Brando described as "a hostile, primitive region—cut off from the niceties of civilization." After two months, the company moved to Marrakesh, where Marlon's relationship with director Gillo Pontecorvo was strained to the breaking point. Director and star disagreed on almost everything—dialogue, retakes, the casting of extras—and their bickering was exacerbated by a language barrier. Pontecorvo was not fluent in English.

"Right now I want to kill Gillo," Brando said to a visiting friend. "I really want to kill him, because he has no fucking feeling for people." Pontecorvo responded in Italian: "Brando is a great artist. He can give more than it is possible for an actor to give. But I never saw an actor so afraid of the camera. And I do not think any artist should be so difficult."

Finally *Burn!* filming ground to a halt after almost eight months. The French-Italian production company filed suit against Marlon for $700,000, claiming his "incomprehensible attitudes" held up shooting. The suit was later dropped.

OPPOSITE: *Burn!* emerged as an uneven film, reflecting the chaos of its production, but Marlon's performance brought him decent reviews for a change. *The Hollywood Reporter:* "Initially, Brando's Englishman is a trifle foppish, sounding like an effete James Mason is lodged like a swallow in the back of his throat. Bearded and blond, he then proceeds to do more in one minute with the character than most actors do in the course of two hours." In keeping with Marlon's last dozen pictures, *Burn!* fizzled at the box office and received scant distribution by United Artists.

As Marlon Brando began his third decade as a film actor, his professional future could not have looked blacker. Most of his performances since the early fifties had not been widely admired, he was considered a troublemaker who was a poor box office risk to boot and he constantly whined about the unworthiness of acting as an occupation, never mind an art.

Apparently his only joy at this time came from his tranquil life in Papeete. He had become deeply involved with various Tahitian organizations concerned with the threat of pollution, overdevelopment of the islands by hotel conglomerates and programs established to teach new farming techniques to the islanders. His relationship with Tarita seemed sound and he was thrilled when she gave birth to a baby daughter, also named Tarita, in February 1970. Marlon's career would hang in limbo for over a year, but he would then be offered a role he couldn't refuse, one that presented him with what he needed most—a challenge.

VI

Comeback

1972–1974

OPPOSITE: A close-up from *The Nightcomers,* the film that marked the beginning of Brando's career resurrection. In sharp contrast to his usual priorities, he signed for this unusual thriller because he was anxious to play the lead, not because of a fabulous salary offer. In fact, he made the picture for no fee whatsoever—agreeing instead to accept a percentage of any profits accrued. This decision to make a film for artistic rather than financial considerations was a telling one, indicating that Marlon was still capable of enthusiasm for his craft when a provocative role turned up.

The Nightcomers established the peculiar genre of the movie "prequel." It is based on characters created by Henry James in his eerie masterpiece *The Turn of the Screw*—filmed in 1961 as *The Innocents.* In the James story, two children on an English estate are haunted by the ghosts of Peter Quint, a rough-hewn Irish groundskeeper whose sexual tastes run to the sadomasochistic, and his lover, the outwardly prim Margaret Jessel. In *The Nightcomers,* screenwriter Michael Hastings speculates on the Quint and Jessel characters prior to their deaths, in an attempt to explain their motivations for terrorizing the children in the original story.

ABOVE RIGHT: A sexually charged scene from *The Nightcomers,* with Brando as Peter Quint and Stephanie Beacham (lately the star of TV's "The Colbys") as Margaret Jessel.

Some comic moments arose during the filming of these bondage-flavored encounters. Beacham is completely deaf in her right ear, and Brando was still frequently using earplugs on the set. Until the two actors became familiar with each other's idiosyncrasies there was a definite lack of communication during some of their most intimate scenes.

In a break from his recent past, Marlon got along well with director Michael Winner and *The Nightcomer*'s supporting cast. Filming on the British locations was completed in a remarkable six weeks.

BELOW RIGHT: With his flawless Irish accent and threatening personality, Marlon's Peter Quint gave *The Nightcomers* its prime distinction. Charming and blustery one minute, taunting and vicious the next, the performance is in some ways too large and complex for the film. But Brando fans welcomed it as an encouraging sign that the actor might be feeling a renewed sense of passion about his career.

Unfortunately, *The Nightcomers* received limited distribution and faded from view quickly. Thankfully, Marlon's next project was already in preparation as he completed *The Nightcomers;* he would be playing the title role in a Paramount production of Mario Puzo's best-selling novel about warring Mafia families, *The Godfather.*

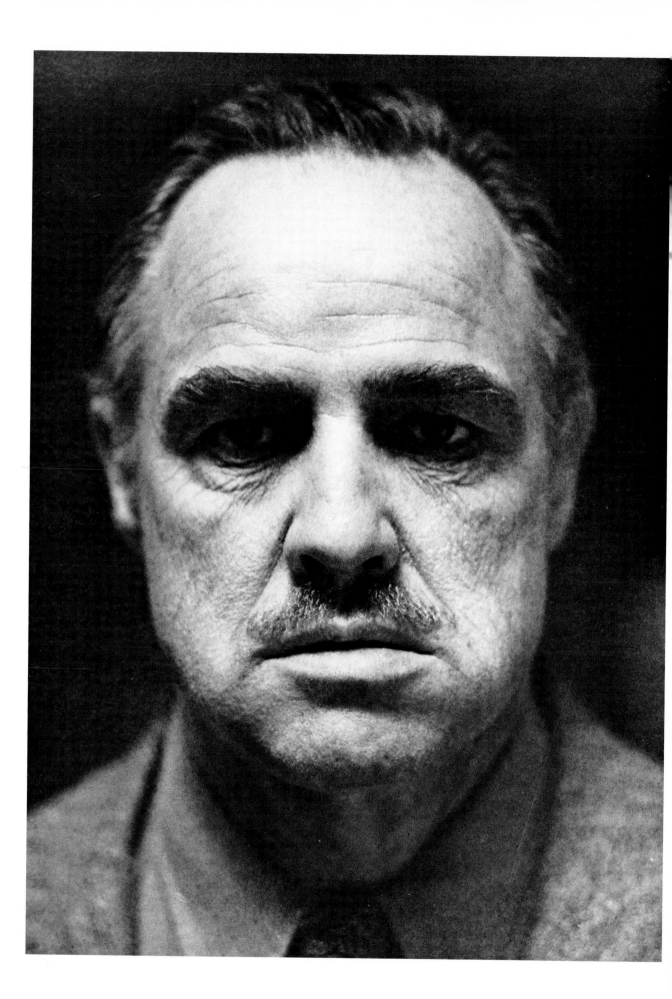

OPPOSITE: The role of aging Don Vito Corleone was not handed to Brando without reservations. Paramount originally wanted Laurence Olivier for the part, and to help convince the studio that he could at least *look* authentic, Marlon, then forty-seven, filmed a brief, unofficial screen test wearing an improvised version of the makeup he would later use in the film.

He darkened his hair and brows, sketched on—and later grew—an "old man's" mustache and stuffed his cheeks with cotton padding to achieve a saggy look. He called the completed effect "the face of a bulldog. Mean-looking, but warm underneath."

Studio executives were impressed with the mini-test, but they were hesitant about casting Brando because of his reputation as a troublemaker and the poor performance at the box office of his last several films. Director Francis Ford Coppola was adamant about casting Marlon, reasoning with producer Robert Evans that his presence in the picture would elevate the performances of the rest of the cast—in view of the "almost mystical" regard in which Brando was held by other actors.

Brando told Evans, "You may have heard a lot of crap about how I misbehaved on pictures. Some of it is true, some of it is not true. But I'll tell you this: I want to play this role. I'll work for it, work hard. It's going to be something special for me." After he agreed to take no salary up front, Brando was signed to play Don Corleone in *The Godfather.*

ABOVE: Joining Marlon in *The Godfather* was a new generation of actors who did indeed idolize their costar. Here Don Corleone is surrounded by his sons; at left is Al Pacino as Michael, to the right of Brando is James Caan as Sonny, the family stud, and John Cazale as Fredo.

Pacino's first scene to be filmed opposite Brando was the bedside vigil Michael keeps for his father following an assassination attempt. "Have you any idea what it is for me to be doing a scene with *him?*" Pacino remarked to a visiting writer. "I sat in theaters when I was a kid, just watching him. Now I'm playing a scene with him. He's God, man."

Midway through *The Godfather* production, there was a move to fire Coppola because of cost overruns. Paramount was nervous about the budget, as the studio had lost money a year earlier on *The Brotherhood,* a similarly themed picture with Kirk Douglas as a Mafia chieftain. Elia Kazan was mentioned as a possible replacement, but when Brando—with all due respect to his old friend Kazan—threatened to walk off the film if such a switch was made, Coppola was wisely retained.

ABOVE LEFT: Relaxing between takes, Marlon toys with a mandolin. Knowing that he was making an important picture that would probably be a smash hit, Brando was in high spirits for most of *The Godfather* filming. He reverted to his old habit of clowning around on the set but with a new twist—when it was least expected, he would suddenly drop his pants, bend over and "moon" the cast and crew. This diversion—sometimes to relieve on-set tensions—was contagious and eventually mooning contests between Brando, Caan and costar Robert Duvall became commonplace.

In a more serious vein, Marlon bent over backward to cooperate with his coworkers on this production. When one sound technician timidly mentioned that he was having trouble understanding Brando, he responded, "Hey, why didn't you tell me? It's no problem. Just tell me and I'll speak more clearly." He never complained about the hour-plus makeup session each morning and he gladly stayed after hours to read offscreen lines to costars for their reaction shots. Friends noticed that he hadn't enjoyed making a movie so much in almost two decades.

BELOW LEFT: *The Godfather* opened for Easter 1972 to adulatory reviews and record-breaking box office business. It did, in fact, establish the tradition of the "event" film, paving the way for such blockbusters as *The Exorcist, Jaws* and *Star Wars.* Theaters playing *The Godfather* had to set up round-the-clock screenings and waiting in line for two or more hours to see the picture became commonplace. Brando was delighted with this success, though he privately groused that he should have made more money from his percentage deal. His final payment was reportedly in the $1.5-million range.

With its flawless performances and shocking violence played against a background of richly hued opulence, *The Godfather* captured the imagination of the public as no gangster saga had since the 1930s. Francis Ford Coppola became the most sought-after director in Hollywood and several cast members, including Pacino and Caan, became overnight stars.

For Marlon, of course, the success of the picture meant true career salvation. Not since *On the Waterfront* had he appeared in a film of such enormous impact. Now, in addition to Terry Malloy's taxi lament, Brando impersonators puffed their cheeks and whispered hoarsely, "We'll make him an offer he can't refuse . . ." in homage to Don Corleone.

For his mesmerizing performance in *The Godfather,* Marlon received his first Academy Award nomination in fifteen years. The film was nominated in ten categories, including "Best Picture." "Best Supporting Actor" nods went to Pacino, Caan and Duvall.

ABOVE: Just prior to the opening of *The Godfather*, Marlon reported to Paris to begin work on his most controversial (and personally taxing) film, *Last Tango in Paris*. He confers here with director Bernardo Bertolucci and costar Maria Schneider.

In its simplest description, *Last Tango* is a character study of Paul, a middle-aged American in Paris who is forced to examine his directionless life following his wife's suicide. He is at his most emotionally vulnerable when he meets Jeanne, a trendy young French girl on the verge of marriage.

Paul and Jeanne engage in a three-day affair that is intensely sexual and impersonal at the same time. When not making love—sometimes violently—they share snippets of their personal histories in stream-of-consciousness monologues. They never exchange names.

Brando had admired Bertolucci's earlier picture *The Conformist* and he was pleased to discover that, unlike past directors, Bertolucci actually *sought* Marlon's opinions and suggestions. Actor and director established a strong trusting bond that helped Brando through some of the film's most difficult scenes. And it was not, as one might expect, the frank sexual moments in *Tango* that gave Marlon the most trouble. It was instead the long monologues in which Paul reflects upon his past that Brando found painful because Bertolucci encouraged him to use his own experiences in these scenes: "My father was a drunk, a screwed-up bar fighter. My mother was also a drunk. My memories as a kid are of being arrested. We lived in a small town, a farming community . . . I can't remember many good things."

ABOVE: Maria Schneider and Marlon in *Last Tango in Paris*. Nineteen-year-old Schneider felt no intimidation in working with Brando. "He's a man who is still a child," she told *Time*. "And a little ambivalent. He feels himself old. All the time he is watching his makeup. Nearly every morning someone has to go out and find him. Without that, he will never arrive for work. He is lazy and also slow. He never knows his words. He improvises. He is a great drinker. We had a sort of rapport, but it wasn't a sexual attraction. For him, it is love that is important. For me, it is life."

Brando did indeed have trouble remembering his lines. For one complicated scene, he requested that his dialogue be written on Schneider's bare behind, where he could refer to it easily.

ABOVE: *Last Tango in Paris* had its first American showing as the closing film of the New York Film Festival on October 14, 1972. *New Yorker* critic Pauline Kael became the picture's greatest champion, declaring that the date of its premiere would go down in film history. "Bertolucci and Brando have altered the face of an art form," Kael wrote in her review. "Who was prepared for that?"

Many critics were unprepared for *Tango*'s sexual explicitness, particularly one coupling in which Paul improvises with a stick of butter as a lubricant for sodomizing Jeanne. If Bertolucci had gotten his way, the picture would have been even steamier. Brando said upon *Tango*'s release: "I didn't like the movie. It was too calculated, designed to make an impact rather than a statement. Bernardo wanted me to screw Maria Schneider on the screen. I told him, 'That's impossible. If that happens, our sex organs become the centerpiece of the film.' He never did agree with me."

Last Tango was not universally hailed. Many found it disturbing if not obscene and it played most successfully in large sophisticated cities. (It ran continuously for four years at one London theater.) There was no disagreement about Brando's performance, however. Following on the heels of *The Godfather*, it reaffirmed Marlon's comeback and brought him another Oscar nomination.

With cover stories in *Time, Life* and *Newsweek*, Brando was clearly back on top, but he hadn't mellowed much. To his credit, the reborn superstar was still a rebel and he would continue to generate controversy.

OPPOSITE: March 27, 1973—Brando wins the "Best Actor" Oscar for his work in *The Godfather*, which was named "Best Picture." The announcement of Marlon's victory was a popular one with the attending audience until Sasheen Littlefeather—seen here after the ceremonies—took the stage on Brando's behalf and refused the award in protest over the treatment in films (and otherwise) of the American Indian.

Loud boos were heard from the audience as Littlefeather read from a lengthy statement prepared by Marlon, which included the comment: "I think awards in this country at this time are inappropriate to be received or given until the condition of the American Indian is drastically altered."

Some were impressed with Brando's snub of the Oscar, but the press was harsh. *Variety* said, "Rudeness has never advanced any cause." "He deeply offended the public and the industry whose sympathy and help he is seeking," wrote *The Hollywood Reporter*. While Sasheen Littlefeather was facing the world press, Marlon was in Wounded Knee, South Dakota, to support the Oglala Sioux Indians in their protest against local job and housing discrimination.

ABOVE: At this 1974 benefit held at the Waldorf-Astoria Hotel in New York, Marlon poses with Dick Cavett and a representative from the American Indian Development Association.

"There is something obscene about the fact that we're dressing up in our monkey suits and inviting a lot of rich people to raise money for the Indians," Brando told the assembled guests and reporters. "It costs a lot to have this thing and we won't get much out of it. But if I had it in my backyard, I don't know if anybody would be there."

Marlon had just taped an appearance on Cavett's talk show, where he was reluctant to discuss anything except the Indian "situation." As he was leaving the television studio, he was confronted by a swarm of aggressive photographers; he ended up slugging one, Ron Galella, who subsequently sued Brando for $500,000. Galella—known for his harassment of Jacqueline Onassis—accepted an out-of-court settlement and always made sure he was photographed wearing a crash helmet when he was stalking Brando in the future.

Because of situations such as this, Marlon again retreated from the spotlight that had been following him since *The Godfather*. His appearances on behalf of Indian issues became less frequent and he returned to the privacy of his Tahitian home.

VII

Recluse
1975–1987

ABOVE: Jack Nicholson and Marlon chat on location for *The Missouri Breaks* in Billings, Montana. Directed by Arthur Penn, this brutal, off-center Western traced the murderous trail of Brando as Robert Lee Clayton, a professional killer hired to track down and eliminate a gang of cattle rustlers led by Nicholson.

For his first film in over three years, Brando seemed to be reverting back to his old policy: "It's a picture everybody is doing for the money," he told Los Angeles *Times* writer Wayne Warga. "Arthur wants to get to his Attica film. I want to get to Tahiti and do some solar, methane and wind environmental experiments."

ABOVE RIGHT: Under the best of circumstances, *The Missouri Breaks* might have proven to be an interesting—if prosaic—Western tale. But as directed by Penn and overacted by its stars, it emerged as an embarrassing flop. With an Irish brogue that was a parody of the one he had assumed in *The Nightcomers*, Marlon delivered a weird, fey performance that left Nicholson groping for a balanced characterization of his own. Penn said at the time, "Nicholson's relationship to Brando—every actor's relationship to Brando—is very complicated. It's like an act of homage just to work with Brando. Every once in a while, Jack would get frustrated by some of the stuff that Marlon was doing. Every once in a while, it would catch him unawares, that's all."

The Missouri Breaks opened in the spring of 1976 to terrible reviews and disappointing public reaction. Fans of Brando and Nicholson did not turn out in sufficient numbers to help the box office and the picture failed to turn a profit. Marlon was lucky to get away with his $1-million-plus salary.

BELOW RIGHT: An amusing candid shot of Nicholson with Brando in one of his goofier getups from *The Missouri Breaks.* Because of the foppish way Marlon had played Robert Lee Clayton, some critics speculated that the character was homosexual. Brando never commented on the subject one way or another, but it was around this time that he made a candid statement about his *personal* sexuality.

"Like a large number of men," he told a French magazine, "I too have had homosexual experiences and I am not ashamed. I've never paid much attention to what people said about me. Deep down I feel a bit ambiguous and I'm not saying that to spite the seven out of ten women who consider me—wrongly perhaps—a sex symbol. Let's say sex is sexless . . . Homosexuality is so much in fashion, it no longer makes news."

Surprisingly, Marlon's revelations did *not* make much news. Though hardly "in fashion," homosexuality was looked on with more tolerance than in the past, and also Brando's days as a fantasy sex image were behind him. In addition, the public had come to expect the unexpected from Marlon. The thought that this most unorthodox of stars had experimented sexually came as no great shock to either his detractors or admirers.

ABOVE: Marlon's next assignment would be for Francis Coppola in *Apocalypse Now*, but prior to the release of that troubled production, Brando was seen in *Superman* playing Jor-El, the father of the title character.

He is seen here with Susannah York as his wife Lara and Lee Quigley as the infant Superboy. With this "popcorn" epic, Brando became the highest-paid actor in the world, earning $3 million for little more than ten minutes of screen time. There were loud complaints in the press about this inflated salary, but producers Alexander and Ilya Salkind stated publicly that Marlon was worth every penny; because of his signing, they were able to raise the money needed to produce the $30 million film.

ABOVE RIGHT: On the *Superman* set in London, Marlon poses with director Richard Donner.

Appearing only in the first moments of *Superman*, Brando had to set the tone for the entire picture by delivering the comic book dialogue with dignity and a sense of reality. As Jor-El, Marlon is a caring father to his infant son whom he sends into space, toward Earth, as his native planet of Krypton is exploding around him. And he looks wonderful with cotton-candy white hair, dressed in elegant flowing robes. Even the extra poundage he was carrying added to his commanding screen presence.

BELOW RIGHT: With its high-tech special effects and solid performances, *Superman* became one of the major hits of 1978 and has spawned three sequels. Brando's salary garnered more space in reviews of the film than did his performance. Some critics were outraged to see so little of Brando for such an inflated fee. "I have a right to get the money I get," he told the London press. "First of all, because I'm not forcing anyone to give it to me. Secondly, I've gained a lot of experience over the years and I don't need the same kind of coaching a newcomer does . . ."

One newcomer, Christopher Reeve (who became a star in the title role of *Superman),* was less impressed with Brando than past costars had been. "I guess," he told the London *Daily Mail,* "he just did the film to pay some debts, buy an island or whatever. But frankly, I found it an anticlimax working with him. He would come in in the morning and be totally out of it. Cold. Reading a paper. The funny little slippers on. Looking like a walrus who had got out of the pool too early."

ABOVE: Brando and Martin Sheen talk between scenes of *Apocalypse Now*, filmed before but released after *Superman*.

Francis Coppola's epic, surreal statement on the Vietnam experience (based loosely on Joseph Conrad's novel *Heart of Darkness) Apocalypse Now* tells of young Captain Willard (Sheen) who is sent on a mission through the heart of the Vietnam jungles to relieve the command of Colonel Kurtz. Obsessed with power, Kurtz has become deranged and taken the war into his own unsteady hands. Brando accepted the Kurtz role after it had been turned down by Jack Nicholson, Robert Redford and Al Pacino.

Reams have been written about Coppola's tremendous difficulty in completing *Apocalypse Now:* Martin Sheen suffered a heart attack during the location shooting in Manila, ferocious typhoons resulted in ruined sets, and tropic diseases took a toll with the crew. The budget sprang from $14 million to over $40 million and the originally scheduled four-month shoot stretched into two years.

For once, Brando escaped blame for the problems on the picture. He was required in Manila for only a month to shoot his scenes, which take place at the end of the film and comprise no more than twenty minutes of screen time.

OPPOSITE: Brando agreed to a head-shaving to play Colonel Kurtz, as Coppola wanted the character to suggest "an enormous malevolent Buddha."

One critic found Brando's performance as Kurtz "full of mystical mumblings and stilted phrasing," but Coppola was wise in choosing him for the small but pivotal role. Kurtz is not sharply defined; we learn little about him, but the sense of mystery he exudes *must* be genuine. By placing Brando in the part, Coppola was able to rely a great deal on the actor's personal charisma to create an indelible screen image. It is less a performance than an artful display of star power at its most potent.

Apocalypse Now, one of the most publicized films of the late seventies, lumbered into theaters in August 1979, over three years after Marlon had signed for the picture. Reviews were mixed, although all agreed that it was a noble undertaking and the film went on to earn an Oscar nomination as the year's "Best Picture."

With *Apocalypse Now* and *Superman* behind him, Brando turned to an unexpected arena for his next acting assignment: television.

ABOVE: Brando's experience with television had been primarily limited to rare talk show appearances. He hadn't acted in the medium since 1950, when he appeared as a favor to a friend in a little-seen NBC teleplay, *Come Out Fighting.*

Thus it was surprising when he signed with producer David Wolper (seen here) to appear as George Lincoln Rockwell, founder of the American Nazi Party, in *Roots II: The Next Generation,* aired in November 1979.

In this sequel to the most popular miniseries ever, *Roots* author Alex Hailey (played by James Earl Jones) spends several minutes interviewing Rockwell for his research. Again, Marlon's screen time was short, but he made the most of it. A fan of *Roots,* Brando had approached Wolper personally about appearing in the sequel, but only if he could play a villain.

"I'm no snob about television," Marlon said. "I think more important things should be done with TV since it reaches a mass audience. If anything, the frivolity should be on the movie screen, where people go if they want escapist entertainment, and television should get down to business with more serious matters."

OPPOSITE: "Marlon Brando is quite good—albeit brief—as Rockwell," said *The Hollywood Reporter.* "He creates a fascinating aura of ignorant arrogance that's torpedoed because the scene isn't allowed to end dramatically—it merely fizzles out."

Fizzle or no, Marlon managed to win an Emmy Award as the year's "Best Supporting Actor" for his performance in *Roots II,* which was a ratings blockbuster. At the time, Marlon was hoping to get a miniseries tracing the history of the American Indian (à la *Roots)* off the ground, but found no interest in such a saga among network heads. At one point, he approached the BBC about the idea, but they too were not interested.

ABOVE: March, 1980—Brando joins Jesse Jackson in a civil rights protest in Dodger Stadium in Los Angeles. Seen less and less frequently at public events, Marlon was irritated when asked how he spent his time away from the camera. "People ask that a lot," he told reporters. "They say, 'What did you do while you took time out?'—as if the rest of my life is taking time out. But the fact is, making *movies* is time out for me because the rest, the nearly complete whole, is what's real for me.

"I'm not an actor and haven't been for years. I'm a human being—hopefully a concerned and somewhat intelligent one—who occasionally acts."

ABOVE RIGHT: Also in 1980, Brando appeared with George C. Scott in his final film to date, *The Formula*, for MGM. Cast as Adam Steiffel, a grasping American oil tycoon, in a muddled mystery thriller about synthetic fuel unearthed from the Nazi era, Marlon adopted a dowdy aging look for his seventy-five-year old character.

Under the direction of John Avildsen *(Rocky)*, Marlon used a "cornpone, down-home drawl" for his characterization and, as with his past few pictures, was on-screen for only a few minutes. The picture was carried by Scott as an investigator.

BELOW RIGHT: Kidded about his elderly appearance in *The Formula*, Brando responded, "One's not allowed to age in this country. Wrinkles, balding and overweight are almost prohibited, particularly for someone in the public eye."

The Formula was not a hit and its stars did not receive good reviews. Of Brando's work *Time* said, "His performance is not truly good—it lacks a real edge of sharpness—but it is often funny, a kind of comment on the heavy-handedness of the film." As usual, Marlon's large salary for *The Formula* came under attack and biographer Gary Carey noted that, "For his last four professional TV and movie appearances, Brando had received close to $10 million for what added up to about thirty minutes of screen time."

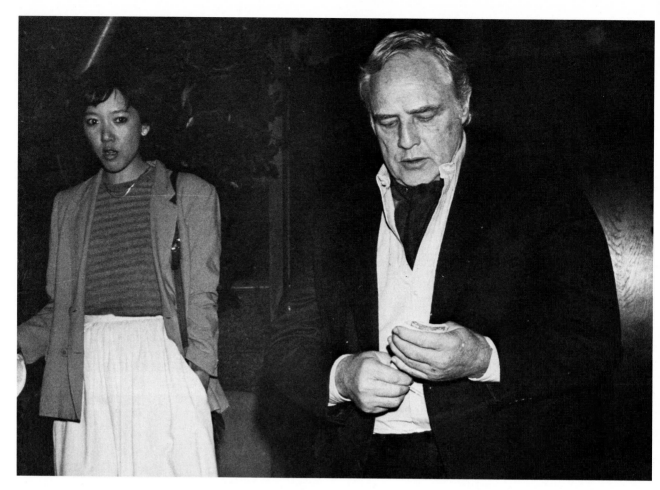

ABOVE: A recent candid shot of Marlon with Yuchico Tsubaki leaving a Los Angeles restaurant. As with all of his personal relationships, Brando kept Miss Tsubaki out of the limelight. Few knew of their romance until 1986, when it was disclosed that they had been together for four years but had decided not to wed in deference to the wishes of Miss Tsubaki's conservative Japanese parents.

As of this writing, Brando is reportedly involved with Caroline Barrett, a Chinese-American who had worked on and off as Marlon's secretary for several years. As usual, Brando has remained mute about these relationships in the press: "I never discuss anyone who hasn't voluntarily put themselves in the public eye. My privacy is constantly being invaded, but why should I do the same to those I care about?"

Indeed, Brando has succeeded in keeping his romances quiet. He was devastated by the media circus surrounding his divorce from Anna Kashfi, and consequently he has never uttered a word about the breakup of his relationship with Tarita—if such a breakup even occurred—and he will definitely not talk about his children for public consumption. This quest for privacy for himself and those he loves will doubtless continue, especially since he is keeping such a low career profile at this time.

OPPOSITE: At sixty-three, Marlon Brando seems less enchanted with his profession than ever. He has been offscreen for seven years and has expressed no interest, publicly at least, in returning to his career. Though he is barraged constantly by offers from our most acclaimed filmmakers, he turns *everything* down. He reportedly still hopes, however, to bring his miniseries about the history of the American Indian to television and has expressed a desire to portray Pablo Picasso in a film biography, but neither of these projects has grown beyond the planning stage.

Although he denies being a recluse, Brando is almost never seen at public events and when he *is* spotted, for example, strolling with Brigitte Bardot on her French estate, driving his Jeep on the California desert, or simply dining out with friends, it is reported in the gossip columns often accompanied by an unflattering photograph. He still travels extensively, dividing most of his time between London, Los Angeles and Tahiti where he has been selling off much of his property.

Will Marlon Brando, credited with singlehandedly redefining screen acting, ever work again? Is there a Stanley Kowalski or Terry Malloy or Don Corleone waiting in the wings to lure him out of retirement? His many admirers clearly hope so, but even if Brando never acts again, his place in theater and film history is assured, and his legend is secure.

PHOTO SOURCES

AP/Wide World Photos: 91
Cecil Beaton photographs courtesy of Sotheby's London: xiv, 9, 67
Bill Chapman Collection: 17, 24, 49, 72
Ralph Dominguez: 138
Globe Photos, Inc.: 46, 51, 81, 97, 125, 136
The Hollywood Gallery: 43, 47, 48, 55, 62, 63, 70, 74, 75, 76, 80, 90, 103, 106, 107, 113, 124
The Kobal Collection: 8, 19, 20, 25, 27, 30, 34, 35, 56
Bruce Mardes: 142
Ralph Osborne: 79
Neal Peters Photo Files: 3, 6, 16, 31, 40, 53, 58, 59, 64, 68, 71, 72, 77, 123, 140

ABOUT THE AUTHOR

Christopher Nickens is the author of pictorial biographies of Natalie Wood, Bette Davis and Elizabeth Taylor. As an illustrator, he has contributed artwork to biographies of Robert Redford, Anne Francis and Barbra Streisand.

Mr. Nickens attended Hollywood High School and Cooper Union University in New York. He is currently working on a book about Greenwich Village.